THE ENTHUSIAST

Field Guide to Poetry

THE ENTHUSIAST

Field Guide to Poetry

Quercus Publishing Plc
21 Bloomsbury Square, London WC1A 2NS

First published in 2007

A catalogue record of this book is available from the British Library

ISBN 1 84724 104 2
ISBN-13 978 1 84724 104 7

Printed and bound in Great Britain by Clays Ltd, St Ives plc

10 9 8 7 6 5 4 3 2 1

To our equals and betters

The Enthusiast
would like to acknowledge everyone
who has helped.

Contents

What is a poem?

Far greater writers than *The Enthusiast* have endeavoured to say what a poem is. The list of contributors to the conversation might include, as a minimal sample: Sappho, Plato, Aristotle, Virgil, Horace, Dante, Sidney, Jonson, Johnson, Hegel, Hölderlin, Wordsworth, Shelley, Keats, Whitman, Mallarmé, Yeats, Rilke, Pound, Trakl, Eliot, Tzara, Auden, and Paul Celan. And Marianne Moore (who 'too disliked it' – poetry that is) and André Breton (who understood that it had to be 'marvellous'), and Martin Heidegger (who found it to be revelatory), and Frank O'Hara (who thought the poem was like a 'call'). And Lorine Niedecker. And Adrienne Rich. And Mina Loy. And Elizabeth Barrett Browning. And Langston Hughes, and Amiri Baraka, and Paul Valéry. Among others.

These writers have spoken with great authority, and in all cases their definitions have won many adherents, and yet by common consent 'the poem' remains a most elusive thing. Even so, and undaunted by the wealth of previous definitions and statements, *The Enthusiast* has – after many years of research – arrived at, or at least glimpsed, a definition of its own:

A poem is an arrangement of words containing possibilities.

This is important. In fact it could hardly be more important. In the corner of the territory with which *The Enthusiast* is familiar – let's call it, for the sake of argument, the over-developed world – there are, roughly speaking, only two possibilities available to people: one is working, and the other is shopping. We work to shop, and we shop in order that we might more effectively work, and we are merrily educating the next generation to do the same. And in case of disruption to the smooth functioning of the work–shop process, we invest enormous amounts of cultural and political energy in closing off alternative possibilities. Here, for instance, are some of the agencies charged with closing off – or down – possibilities for people: schools, universities, ministries of state, firms of accountants, firms of auditors, advertising agencies, banks; focus groups, research councils, funding bodies, corporations; shops, workplaces, television. So successful, in fact, has the shut-down operation been of late that it is difficult, now, to think of any alternatives to working and shopping, and even when we do, before we know it, they've somehow reappeared as more of the same: more working, more shopping, more of both. Which is why, as *The Enthusiast* sees it – and as much as ever – we need the possibilities of the poem.

As a highly charged arrangement of words – already, you'll notice, we're qualifying the definition – a poem presents multiple possibilities, possibilities ranging over numerous fields. (Which is to say, in passing, that this book is not, as the title might imply, a collection of data, but rather a foray into poetry's various fields.) Poetry, that is, as an excitement in language, opens up possibilities for, among other aspects of human existence: love, sex, death, eating, thinking, imagining, interpreting, believing, doubting, protesting and knowing. Poems, in their restlessness, offer previously unimagined ways of talking and relating. They offer new ways of being intimate; new ways, dare one say it, of seeing. But – and here's the 'but' – it is strictly as a form of words that they do this. A poem, let us say it again, is an arrangement of *words* containing possibilities. In words used as well as the poet uses them, new possibilities arise. Words closed down are merely tokens. Words opened up are resources for living. This book is a guide to the possibilities of the poem.

The question is, how are the poem's possibilities to be released?

The first thing to say here is that poems, invariably, are opened up by other poems. The poems in this book have been gathered over many years. They are not representative of any specific period, nor of any given philosophy, type or genre. They have been arranged in such a way that they might show each other off. The book has beginnings and middles and ends, though it isn't absolutely necessary to read it in that way. What the book believes very strongly, however, is that poems are, among other things, commentaries on other poems, that poems are readings, that poems enable the possibilities of other poems.

But readers read poems also, of course. And with each good reading of the poem a new possibility emerges. You will perhaps note another qualification there; the qualification is *good*. Our definition, you'll remember – 'A poem is an arrangement of words containing possibilities' – points strongly to the word 'containing'. Poems contain possibilities, but, to some degree, those meanings are *contained*, where contained means not infinite. Not all readings are possible. Poems are not *all* possible things. A poem's meaning, at any given moment, is a matter of emphasis. A thoughtful emphasis – a good reading – is often a pressure placed on a particular phrase or word. This book's annotations are, therefore, a series of emphases. What the book encourages is a readerly involvement: a thoughtful pressing against the poem's words: a palpation.

So here's what we wanted to do. As contributors to *The Enthusiast*, and as long-time readers of poetry, we wanted to come up with a book that presented a full sense of the possibilities and the pleasures of the form we know as the poem. We wanted to frame the poems we'd grown to appreciate in such a way that they could exist as poems. We wanted to indicate the things they might be thought to say in the sure knowledge that they say other things as well.

We wanted, as we set them out, to unburden the poems of the poet. Not that the emphases given might not, at times, be biographical, or historical, or geographic, or otherwise to do with context. What we wanted to show, however – and in this we salute Monsieur Breton – is that poems offer worlds all of their own, worlds as yet only partly realized.

What follows here, then, is neither working nor shopping. Nor is it a manual. It is, rather, a conversation on the possibilities of poems. Some of the conversationalists you will have heard of already. Some you will want to hear of again. Some not. Some of the contributions are whole poems, some are extracts and samples; some are barely poems at all; some are reflections on poetry. Some of the reflections are dense, and some of them are clear. All, we are quite certain – *quite certain* – are illuminating. And throughout, at the bottom of the page – in the margins – you will hear *The Enthusiast* contributing also, as best we can, and as best we know how.

As for you, we have no idea who you are, and to be honest we have no desire to. We put this book together for people who are better and more energetic than ourselves.

Even as we speak the shops are opening

                    the range of options closing down.

It is a good moment for the possibilities of the poem.

Beginnings

1 The following seem to be the chief difficulties of criticism or, at least, those which we shall have most occasion to consider here:-

A First must come the difficulty of *making out the plain sense* of poetry. The most disturbing and impressive fact brought out by this experiment is that a large proportion of average-to-good (and in some cases, certainly, devoted) readers of poetry frequently and repeatedly *fail to understand it*, both as a statement and as an expression. They fail to make out its prose sense, its plain, overt meaning, as a set of ordinary intelligible, English sentences, taken quite apart from any further poetic significance. And equally, they misapprehend its feeling, its tone and its intention. They would travesty it in a paraphrase. [...] It is not confined to one class of readers; not only those whom we would suspect fall victims. Nor is it only the most abstruse poetry which so betrays us. In fact to set down, for once, the brutal truth, no immunity is possessed on any occasion, not by the most reputable scholar, from this or any of these critical dangers.

B Parallel to, and not unconnected with, these difficulties of interpreting the meaning are the difficulties of *sensuous apprehension*. Words in sequence have a form to the mind's ear and the mind's tongue and larynx, even when silently read. They have a movement and may have a rhythm. The gulf is wide between a reader who naturally and immediately perceives this form and movement [...] and another reader, who either ignores it or has to build it up laboriously with finger-counting, table tapping and the rest; this difference has most far-reaching effects.

C Next may come those difficulties that are connected with the place of *imagery*, principally visual imagery, in poetic reading. They arise in part from the incurable fact that we differ immensely in our capacity to visualise, and to produce imagery of the other senses. Also, the importance of our imagery as a whole, as well as of some pet particular type of image, in our mental lives varies surprisingly. Some minds can do nothing and get nowhere without images; others seem to be able to do everything and get anywhere, reach any and every state of thought and feeling without making use of them. Poets on the whole (though by no means all poets always) may be suspected of exceptional imaging capacity, and some readers are constitutionally prone to stress the place of imagery in reading, to pay great attention to it, and even to judge the value of the poetry by the images it excites in them. But images are erratic things; lively images aroused in one mind need have no similarity to the equally lively images stirred by the same line of poetry in another, and neither set need have anything to do with any images which may have existed in the poet's mind. Here is a troublesome source of critical deviations.

D Thirdly, and more obviously, we have to note the powerful very persuasive influence of *mnemonic irrelevancies*. These are the misleading effects of the reader's being reminded of some personal scene or adventure, erratic associations, the interference of emotional reverberations from a past which may have nothing to do with the poem. Relevance is not an easy notion to define or to apply, though some instances of irrelevant intrusions are among the simplest of all accidents to diagnose.

E More puzzling and more interesting are the critical traps that surround what may be called *Stock Responses*. These have their opportunity whenever a poem seems to, or does, involve views and emotions already fully prepared in the reader's mind, so that what happens appears to be more of the reader's doing than the poet's. The button is pressed, and then the author's work is done, for immediately the record starts playing in quasi- (or total) independence of the poem which is supposed to be its origin or instrument.

Whenever this lamentable redistribution of the poet's and the reader's share in the labour of poetry occurs, or is in danger of occurring, we require to be especially on our guard. Every kind of injustice may be committed as well by those who just escape as by those who are caught.

F *Sentimentality* is a peril that needs less comment here. It is a question of the due measure of response. This over-facility in certain emotional directions is the Scylla whose Charybdis is—

G *Inhibition*. This, as much as Sentimentality, is a positive phenomenon, though less studied until recent years and somewhat masked under the title of Hardness of Heart. But neither can well be considered in isolation.

H *Doctrinal Adhesions* presents another troublesome problem. Very much poetry—religious poetry may be instanced—seems to contain or imply views and beliefs, true or false, about the world. If this be so, what bearing has the truth-value of the views upon the worth of the poetry? Even if it be not so, if the beliefs are not really contained or implied, but only seem so to a non-poetical reading, what should be the bearing of the reader's conviction, if any, upon his estimate of the poetry? Has poetry anything to say; if no, why not, and if so, how? Difficulties at this point are a fertile source of confusion and erratic judgment.

I Passing now to a different order of difficulties, the effects of *technical presuppositions* have to be noted. When something has once been done in a certain fashion we tend to expect similar things to be done in the future in the same fashion, and are disappointed or do not recognise them if they are done differently. Conversely, a technique which has shown its ineptitude for one purpose tends to become discredited for all. Both are cases of mistaking means for ends. Whenever we attempt to judge poetry from outside by technical details we are putting means before ends, and —such is our ignorance of cause and effect in poetry—we shall be lucky if we do not make even worse blunders. We have to avoid judging pianists by their hair.

J Finally, *general critical preconceptions* (prior demands made upon poetry as a result of theories—conscious or unconscious—about its nature and value), intervene endlessly, as the history of criticism shows only too well, between the reader and the poem. Like an unlucky dietetic formula they may cut him off from what he is starving for, even when it is at his very lips.

I.A. RICHARDS, *Practical Criticism* (1929)

2 Compare and contrast:

ἐν ἀρχῇ ἐποίησεν ὁ θεὸς τὸν οὐρανὸν καὶ τὴν γῆν

ἡ δὲ γῆ ἦν ἀόρατος καὶ ἀκατασκεύαστος καὶ σκότος ἐπάνω
τῆς ἀβύσσου καὶ πνεῦμα θεοῦ ἐπεφέρετο ἐπάνω τοῦ ὕδατος

καὶ εἶπεν ὁ θεός γενηθήτω φῶς καὶ ἐγένετο φῶς

In the beginning God created the heaven and the earth.
And the earth was without form, and void; and darkness
was upon the face of the deep. And the Spirit of God
moved upon the face of the waters. And God said, Let
there be light: and there was light.
(THE BIBLE, Genesis 1:1–3)

In the beginning God created the heavens and the earth.
Now the earth was formless and empty, darkness was over
the surface of the deep, and the Spirit of God was
hovering over the waters. And God said, Let there be
light, and there was light.

In the beginning God created the heavens and the earth.
The earth was formless and void, and darkness was over
the surface of the deep, and the Spirit of God was moving
over the surface of the waters. Then God said, "Let there
be light"; and there was light.

First off, nothing. No light, no time, no substance, no
matter. Second off, God starts it all up and WHAP! Stuff
everywhere! The cosmos in chaos: no shape, no form, no
function – just darkness ... total. And floating above it all,
God's Holy Spirit, ready to play. Day one: Then God's
voice booms out, 'Lights!' and, from nowhere, light
floods the skies and 'night' is swept off the scene.

Au commencement, Dieu créa les cieux et la terre. La terre
était informe et vide: il y avait des ténèbres à la surface de

l'abîme, et l'esprit de Dieu se mouvait au-dessus des eaux.
Dieu dit: Que la lumière soit! Et la lumière fut.

Au commencement, Dieu créa le ciel et la terre. Or, la
terre était alors informe et vide. Les ténèbres couvraient
l'abîme, et l'Esprit de Dieu planait au-dessus des eaux. Et
Dieu dit alors:
—Que la lumière soit!
Et la lumière fut.

Am Anfang schuf Gott Himmel und Erde. Und die Erde
war wüst und leer, und es war finster auf der Tiefe; und
der Geist Gottes schwebte auf dem Wasser. Und Gott
sprach: Es werde Licht! und es ward Licht.

Nel principio DIO creò i cieli e la terra. La terra era
informe e vuota e le tenebre coprivano la faccia dell'
abisso; e lo Spirito di DIO aleggiava sulla superficie delle
acque. Poi DIO disse: "Sia la luce!" E la luce fu.

Begyndelsen skabte Gud Himmelen og Jorden. Og Jorden
var øde og tom, og der var Mørke over Verdensdybet. Men
Guds Ånd svævede over Vandene. Og Gud sagde: "Der
blive Lys!" Og der blev Lys.

Dios, en el principio,
    creó los cielos y la tierra.
La tierra era un caos total,
    las tinieblas cubrían el abismo,
y el Espíritu de Dios iba y venía
    sobre la superficie de las aguas.
Y dijo Dios: «¡Que exista la luz!»
    Y la luz llegó a existir.

I begynnelsen skapte Gud himmelen og jorden. Og
jorden var øde og tom, og det var mørke over det store
dyp, og Guds Ånd svevde over vannene. Da sa Gud: Det
bli lys! Og det blev lys.

Quando Deus começou criando o firmamento e a Terra, esta era de início um caos e como uma massa amorfa, com o Espírito de Deus planando sobre os vapores que enchiam as trevas. Então Deus disse: Haja luz. E a luz apareceu.

فِي الْبَدْءِ خَلَقَ اللهُ السَّمَاوَاتِ وَالأَرْضَ،

وَإِذْ كَانَتِ الأَرْضُ مُشَوَّشَةً وَمُقْفِرَةً

وَتَكْتَنِفُ الظُّلْمَةُ وَجْهَ الْمِيَاهِ، وَإِذْ كَانَ

رُوحُ اللهِ يُرَفْرِفُ عَلَى سَطْحِ الْمِيَاهِ،

أَمَرَ اللهُ: «لِيَكُنْ نُورٌ». فَصَارَ نُورٌ،

And so we begin:

3 N. *beginning*, birth, rise (**see** *origin*); infancy, babyhood 130 *youth*, 126 *newness*; primitiveness 127 *oldness*; commencement; onset 295 *arrival*; emergence 445 *appearance*; incipience, inception, inchoation, institution, constitution, foundation, establishment 156 *causation*; origination, invention 484 *discovery*; creation 164 *production*; innovation 21 *originality*; initiative, démarche; exordium, introduction, curtain-raiser 66 *prelude*; alpha, first letter, initial; head, heading, headline, caption 547 *label*; title page, prelims, front matter; van, front, forefront 237 *front*; dawn 128 *morning*; running in, teething troubles, growing pains; first blush, first glance, first sight, first impression, first lap, first round, first stage; early stages, early days, incunabula; primer, outline; rudiments, elements, first principles, alphabet, ABC; leading up to 289 *approach*; outbreak, onset 712 *attack*; debutante, starter 538 *beginner*; precedent 66 *precursor*; preliminaries 669 *preparation*.

From *Roget's Thesaurus*

4 Another beginning:

Of man's first disobedience, and the fruit
Of that forbidden tree, whose mortal taste
Brought death into the world, and all our woe,
With loss of Eden, till one greater man
Restore us, and regain the blissful seat,
Sing heavenly Muse, that on the secret top
Of Oreb, or of Sinai, didst inspire
That shepherd, who first taught the chosen seed,
In the beginning how the heavens and earth
Rose out of chaos: or if Sion hill
Delight thee more, and Siloa's brook that flowed
Fast by the oracle of God; I thence
Invoke thy aid to my adventurous song,
That with no middle flight intends to soar
Above the Aonian mount, while it pursues
Things unattempted yet in prose or rhyme.

JOHN MILTON, *Paradise Lost*, Book 1, ll.1–16 (1674)

The opening lines of Milton's *Paradise Lost*: the most purely outrageous and arrogant 16 lines of verse in the English language, from one of the most purely outrageous and arrogant of English writers.

Milton claims that his work 'pursues / Things unattempted yet in prose or rhyme'.

The Milton scholar David Daiches asks, rightly, 'Unattempted even in the Bible? [...] Unattempted in English literature?'

Whichever.

Milton's pursuit is nothing less than the taste of mortality.

And his mode? An 'adventurous song'.

adventure n. an unusual, exciting, and daring experience. [ORIGIN L. *adventurus* 'about to happen', from *advenire* 'arrive', from *ad-* to + *venire* come.]

Milton has made a beginning.

5 **And to begin again, this time in America:**

You, whoever you are!
You, daughter or son of England!
You of the mighty Slavic tribes and empires! you Russ in
  Russia!
You dim-descended, black, divine-souled African, large,
  fine-headed, nobly-form'd, superbly destined, on
  equal terms with me!

You Norwegian! Swede! Dane! Icelander! you Prussian!
You Spaniard of Spain! you Portuguese!
You Frenchwoman and Frenchman of France!
You Belge! you liberty-lover of the Netherlands! (you
  stock whence I myself have descended;)
You sturdy Austrian! you Lombard! Hun! Bohemian!
  farmer of Styria!
You neighbour of the Danube!
You working-man of the Rhine, the Elbe, or the Weser!
  you working-woman too!
You Sardinian! you Bavarian! Swabian! Saxon! Wallachian!
  Bulgarian!
You Roman! Neapolitan! you Greek!
You lithe matador in the arena at Seville!
You mountaineer living lawlessly on the Taurus or
  Caucasus!
You Bokh horse-herd, watching your mares and stallions
  feeding!
You beautiful-bodied Persian, at full speed in the saddle,
  shooting arrows to the mark!
You Chinaman and Chinawoman of China! you Tartar of
  Tartary!
You women of the earth subordinated at your tasks!
You Jew journeying in your old age through every risk to
  stand once on Syrian ground!
You other Jews waiting in all lands for your Messiah!
You thoughtful Armenian, pondering by some stream of
  the Euphrates! you peering amid the ruins of Nineveh!
  you ascending Mount Ararat!
You foot-worn pilgrim welcoming the far-away sparkle of
  the minarets of Mecca!

You sheiks along the stretch from Suez to Bab-el-mandeb,
    ruling your families and tribes!
You olive-grower tending your fruit on fields of Nazareth,
    Damascus, or Lake Tiberias!
You Thibet trader on the wide inland, or bargaining in the
    shops of Lassa!
You Japanese man or woman! You liver in Madagascar,
    Ceylon, Sumatra, Borneo!
All you continentals of Asia, Africa, Europe, Australia,
    indifferent of place!
All you on the numberless islands of the archipelagos of
    the sea!
And you of centuries hence, when you listen to me!
And you, each and everywhere, whom I specify not, but
    include just the same!
Health to you! good will to you all, from me and America
    sent.

Each of us inevitable;
Each of us limitless, each of us with his or her right upon
    the earth;
Each of us allowed the eternal purports of the earth;
Each of us here as divinely as any is here.

WALT WHITMAN, 'Salut Au Monde!', Section 11 (1856)

Whitman begins at the beginning; or at least, at the beginning of language. Here he is, using words as if for the first time: 'You', he chants, 'All' he chants, 'And' and 'Each'. These are elements, the particles, out of which the poem is made.

And so are we: you, all and each. He names us, and incorporates us, into the body of his poem. But do we accept him? Do we wish to be embraced by Walt Whitman? And to accept him, must we accept America? Are we grateful to him for his salute?

'I have the kiss of Walt Whitman still on my lips,' wrote Oscar Wilde.

6　For as this appalling ocean surrounds the verdant land, so in the soul of man there lies one insular Tahiti, full of peace and joy, but encompassed by all the horrors of the half known life. God keep thee! Push not off from that isle, thou canst never return!

HERMAN MELVILLE, *Moby-Dick*, Chapter 58 (1851)

Herman Melville was a novelist. Herman Melville was a poet. In *Moby-Dick* he was writing an epic of possibility: in which Ishmael, who survives to tell the tale, explores great possibilities of human action and experience; and Ahab, in his single-mindedness, works to close them down.

Like Whitman, Melville repeats himself. Here, as in Whitman, he repeats 'all': except that his 'all' is, in part, 'appalling'; the appalling 'all' of Whitman's mass.

Melville, that is, cautions against self-abandonment. (He is, remember, a novelist. No novelist self-abandons.) He holds an 'I' – an isle – up against Whitman's 'You'.

Ishmael, in his adventurous song, retains a certain caution: 'Push not off from that isle, thou canst never return!'

7 The cultivation of poetry is never more to be desired than at periods when, from an excess of the selfish and calculating principle, the accumulation of the materials of external life exceed the quantity of the power of assimilating them to the internal laws of human nature.

PERCY BYSSHE SHELLEY, *A Defence of Poetry* (1821)

That'd be now, then.

8 THERE are the Alps. What is there to say about them?
They don't make sense. Fatal glaciers, crags cranks climb,
jumbled boulder and weed, pasture and boulder, scree,
et l'on entend, maybe, *le refrain joyeux et leger.*
Who knows what the ice will have scraped on the rock it
    is smoothing?

There they are, you will have to go a long way round
if you want to avoid them.
It takes some getting used to. There are the Alps,
fools! Sit down and wait for them to crumble!

BASIL BUNTING, 'On the Fly-Leaf of Pound's Cantos' (1949)

Basil Bunting is writing in response to Ezra Pound's *Cantos*.

**The Cantos, Bunting asserts, are no more questionable than the
Alps. Note the redundancy of the question, 'What is there to say
about them?'**

What is there to say about them? What is there to ask?

**Of course, Bunting does say something about them, and he does
have a question in mind. How, the poem asks, rhetorically, does
one become familiar with something, with a person, or a mountain,
or a poem? One doesn't get to know a mountain by asking 'why'?
One first acknowledges that the mountain is there. One climbs,
and one clambers, among the boulders, and the scree.**

**Wordsworth identified mountains with the sublime. Bunting shows
how language has become the sublime. In *The Cantos* the sublime
is to be found in *words*. Or rather in writing, in great acts of
linguistic accumulation. Pound's *Cantos*, Bunting notes, are acts
of language – piling up.**

**(There are many other things to say about Pound's vast poem, of
course, and other questions to be put. The poem contains anti-
semitism, for example: Pound was a vociferous anti-semite. This
certainly requires questioning – see No. 41.)**

The Cantos are 'the Alps'.

You may wish to avoid them.

But you'd have to go a long way round.

9   There is another road, besides those we have mentioned, which leads to sublimity. What and what manner of road is this? Zealous imitation of the great historians and poets of the past. That is the aim, dear friend, and we must hold to it with all our might. For many are carried away by the inspiration of another. [...] From the natural genius of those old writers there flows into the hearts of their admirers as it were an emanation from the mouth of holiness. Inspired by this, even those who are not easily moved by the divine afflatus share the enthusiasm of these others' grandeurs. Was Herodotus alone 'Homeric in the highest'? No, there was Stesichorus at a still earlier date and Archilochus too, and above all others Plato, who has irrigated his style with ten thousand runnels from the great Homeric spring.

LONGINUS, *On the Sublime*, XIII, tr. T.S. Dorsch

The phrase here is: 'share the enthusiasm'. This, like Longinus, we take to be a central function of poetry. Whatever the 'enthusiasm' of poetry is, it has to be shared.

(The Earl of Shaftesbury, writing about enthusiasm, defined it as 'an itch to impart'.)

Marianne Moore, who showed her enthusiasm for other writers by quoting them, explained her borrowings thus: 'If I wanted to say something and somebody had said it ideally, then I'd take it but I'd give the person the credit for it. That's all there is to it. If you are charmed by an author, I think it's a very strange and invalid imagination that doesn't long to share it. Somebody else should read it, don't you think?'

Yes. Somebody else should read it, indeed, and the imagination that wants to keep things to itself *is* invalid.

The shared enthusiasm, for all its dangers, one might think of as the poet's gift (see No. 134).

So:

10 Mr. Zukofsky: - In objects which men made and used, people live again. The touch of carving to the hand revivifies the hand that made it. Old wood and weathered polychrome once painted over it—the means of past industry.

Looking at a ship's figurehead of which the idea has been oversimplified only to appear as of today, we wonder how this *thing* could have faded so quickly from men's minds, forgetting that we probably had no opportunity to see it before.

For old things are lost, destroyed, stored away in attics and cellars, sold—accumulate the dust of antique shops and museum cases. Only an enterprise like "The Index of American Design" can bring them back to the people.

As pictures, yes, and as facts. They still exist, because they existed. And because rendering the truths they were to the people who made and used them becomes part of the factual material of the artist's drawing.

A drawing of a ship's figurehead becomes a guide not only to all ships' figureheads that preceded it, but a reason for creating sculpture in our time. It ceases to be a museum piece or a collector's item as soon as the form and color of the drawing help to circulate its image among people. They *must* admire, and demand an effort from contemporary art that will yield a comparable pleasure to the living.

LOUIS ZUKOFSKY, Broadcast No.1: 'The Henry Clay Figurehead'
(16 November 1939), *A Useful Art: Essays and Radio Scripts on American Design*, ed. Kenneth Sherwood

You could substitute here the word 'poem' for 'ship's figurehead'.

And '*The Enthusiast Field Guide to Poetry*' for 'The Index of American Design'.

And 'poetry' for 'sculpture'.

'Help to circulate its image among people'

remains the same:

11

What thoughts I have of you tonight, Walt Whitman, for I walked down the sidestreets under the trees with a headache self-conscious looking at the full moon.

In my hungry fatigue, and shopping for images, I went into the neon fruit supermarket, dreaming of your enumerations!

What peaches and what penumbras! Whole families shopping at night! Aisles full of husbands! Wives in the avocados, babies in the tomatoes!—and you, García Lorca, what were you doing down by the watermelons?

I saw you, Walt Whitman, childless, lonely old grubber, poking among the meats in the refrigerator and eyeing the grocery boys.

I heard you asking questions of each: Who killed the pork chops? What price bananas? Are you my Angel?

I wandered in and out of the brilliant stacks of cans following you, and followed in my imagination by the store detective.

We strode down the open corridors together in our solitary fancy tasting artichokes, possessing every frozen delicacy, and never passing the cashier.

Where are we going, Walt Whitman? The doors close in an hour. Which way does your beard point tonight?

(I touch your book and dream of our odyssey in the supermarket and feel absurd.)

Will we walk all night through the solitary streets? The trees add shade to shade, lights out in the houses, we'll both be lonely.

Will we stroll dreaming of the lost America of love past blue automobiles in driveways, home to our silent cottage?

Ah, dear father, graybeard, lonely old courage-teacher, what America did you have when Charon quit poling his ferry and you got out on a smoking bank and stood watching the boat disappear on the black waters of Lethe?

ALLEN GINSBERG, 'A Supermarket in California' (1955)

So, shopping: 'A Supermarket in California'.

'Whole families,' Ginsberg explains, 'shopping at night!'

And among the families, Whitman, 'asking questions of each'. Humdrum questions: 'Who killed the pork chops? What price bananas?' And questions – in their high-flown-ness, in their expectation of something more – insisting on greater possibilities. 'Are you,' Whitman/Ginsberg asks, 'my Angel?'

In 'London, 1802', Wordsworth calls upon Milton to make good again the 'English dower of inward happiness':

> Milton! Thou shouldst be living at this hour:
> England hath need of thee: she is a fen
> Of stagnant waters: altar, sword, and pen,
> Fireside, the heroic wealth of hall and bower,
> Have forfeited their ancient English dower
> Of inward happiness.

Ginsberg, writing in the 1950s – after the war in Korea, and before the war in Vietnam, in the shadow of McCarthyism – calls upon Whitman likewise to make good. These – Wordsworth's, Ginsberg's – are poems of homage and appeal, calling upon the power and resources of some other, earlier poet.

Acts of homage and appeal can be embarrassing: '(I touch your book and dream of our odyssey in the supermarket and feel absurd.)'

But Allen Ginsberg wants us to be embarrassed by the presence of Walt Whitman.

'I have the kiss of Walt Whitman still on my lips' (see No. 5).

12 Then said he unto me: Prophesy unto the wind, prophesy, son of man, and say unto the wind, Thus said the Lord God; Come from the four winds, O breath, and breathe upon these slain, that they may live.

THE BIBLE, Ezekiel 37:9

Witness Ginsberg. Witness Wordsworth.

13 No radiant angel came across the gloom with a clear message for her. In those times, as now, there were human beings who never saw angels or heard perfectly clear messages. Such truth as came to them was brought confusedly in the voices and deeds of men not at all like the seraphs of unfailing wing and piercing vision [...]. The helping hands stretched out to them were the hands of men who stumbled and often saw dimly, so that these beings unvisited by angels had no other choice than to grasp that stumbling guidance along the path of reliance and action which is the path of life, or else to pause in loneliness and disbelief, which is no path, but the arrest of inaction and death.

GEORGE ELIOT, *Romola*, Chapter 36 (1863)

George Eliot is right (just as Allen Ginsberg was right): 'The path of reliance and action [...] is the path of life.' And there are not 'perfectly clear messages'. And the truth is often confusedly brought. And the poet who claims otherwise is suspect.

14

Poetry is not like reasoning, a power to be exerted according to the determination of the will. A man cannot say, 'I will compose poetry.'

PERCY BYSSHE SHELLEY, *A Defence of Poetry* (1821)

Actually, a man can say 'I will compose poetry.' And he does. And she does. It is a Romantic myth, one that Shelley says he subscribes to, to suggest otherwise.

And nor is poetry – as Shelley suggests – to be so readily differentiated from 'reasoning'. A poem is an argument. It is a particular way of arguing, but it is an argument – witness 'A Supermarket in California' – nonetheless.

Shelley knew this. For sure. His poems argue all the time. What he perhaps had in mind was the need for the poet not to be *determined*. But 'determined', as with all things, cuts both ways. It is a double-edged sword. Witness:

15 What basic propositions are indispensable when one begins poetical work?

First thing. The presence of a problem in society, the solution of which is conceivable only in poetical terms. A social command. (An interesting theme for special study would be the disparity between the social command and actual commissions.)

Second thing. An exact knowledge, or rather intuition, of the desires of your class (or the group you represent) on the question, i.e. a standpoint from which to take aim.

Third thing. Materials. Words. Fill your storehouse constantly, fill the granaries of your skull with all kinds of words, necessary, expressive, rare, invented, renovated and manufactured.

Fourth thing. Equipment for the plant and tools for the assembly line. A pen, a pencil, a typewriter, a telephone, an outfit for your visits to the doss-house, a bicycle for your trips to the publishers, a table in good order, an umbrella for writing in the rain, a room measuring the exact number of paces you have to take when you're working, connection with a press agency to send you information on questions of concern to the provinces and so on and so forth, and even a pipe and cigarettes.

Fifth thing. Skills and techniques of handling words, extremely personal things, which come only with years of daily work: rhymes, metres, alliteration, images, lowering of style, pathos, closure, finding a title, layout, and so on and so forth.

For example: the social task may be to provide the words for a song for the Red Army men on their way to the Petersburg front. The purpose is to defeat Yudenich. The material is words from the vocabulary of soldiers. The tools of production – a pencil stub. The device – the rhymed *chastushka*.

VLADIMIR MAYAKOVSKY, *How Are Verses Made?* (1926), tr. G.M. Hyde

This is brilliant. Mayakovsky is refuting Shelley.

(He does not know he is refuting Shelley, but he is: he does.)

Mayakovsky, writing in revolutionary Russia, emphasizes the productive process.

He is writing about materials, words, about the need for the progressive poet to 'fill the granaries of your skull with all kinds of words'.

His recommendations to the bourgeois poet are deadly serious and self-explanatory.

Except perhaps for *chastushka*.

A *chastushka* is the Russian equivalent of a limerick.

16 Ah, this is my ambition indeed:
To rise up among all the insipid, unsalted, rabbity,
    endlessly hopping people

And sing a great song of our Alba bheadarrach
— An exuberant, fustigating, truculent, polysyllabic
Generous, eccentric, and incomparably learned song
And so bring fresh laurels to deck the brows
Of Alba bheadarrach is Alba-nuadhaichte, ath-leasaichte,
    is ath-bheothaicte.

HUGH MACDIARMID, 'My Ambition' (1938)

bheadarrach: beloved
is: and
ath-nuadhaichte: newborn
ath-leasaichte: newly improved
ath-bheothaicte: new come to life.

Hugh MacDiarmid, achieving his ambition: 'An exuberant, fustigating, truculent, polysyllabic / Generous, eccentric, and incomparably learned song'.

Adventurous song. Noble ambition.

A poem, a good poem, is invariably a statement of ambition: the ambition of the poet; his or her ambition for the person reading the poem.

'Of Alba bheadarrach is Alba-nuadhaichte, ath-leasaichte, is ath-bheothaicte.'

The poem says several things, but through all of them it says one thing: 'My Ambition' *is* a poem.

17   All languages, both learned and mother tongues, be gotten, and gotten only by Imitation. For as ye use to hear, so ye learn to speak: if ye hear no other, ye speak not your self: and whom ye only hear, of them ye only learn.

And therefore, if ye would speak as the best and wisest do, ye must be conversant, where the best and wisest are.

ROGER ASCHAM, *The Schoolmaster* (1570)

This is perhaps an unnecessary reminder.

But it is a reminder nonetheless.

18 Old houses were scaffolding once
and workmen whistling.

T.E.HULME, 'Images' (1912)

This seems to relate to some of the previous poems and statements.

A self-confessed 'philosophic amateur', a non-smoking teetotalling radical Tory, a poet who published only a handful of poems (of which 'Images' is one, in its entirety) and called them his 'Complete Poetical Works', who despised 'the state of slush in which we have the misfortune to live', who was thrown out of Cambridge University not once but twice, who was never happier than when organizing some kind of philosophical club or involving himself in an argument, and who kept a brass knuckleduster designed for him by Gaudier-Brzeska in order to pleasure his lover, T.E. Hulme was what one might call a pushful sort of a character. He was an enthusiast. His middle name was Ernest, he was blown to pieces while manning a gun on the Belgian coast in 1917, a few weeks after his 34th birthday, and he loved boiled sweets and sex.

The attraction of Hulme's various writings, according to his biographer Robert Ferguson, is that 'of overhearing someone in the actual process of thinking'. Is this right? To hear someone in the actual 'actual process of thinking' might sound something like this: 'Damn. Shit. Plinky-plonky-plink', a kind of a cross between musique concrète and Eminem. A better way of saying it might be that Hulme attended to the central moral and aesthetic questions and difficulties, and attempted to write about them clearly, without bluffing or condescension. Compared to many of the other, typical self-preening intellectuals of the period, his writing seems almost pre-philosophical and ur-poetic. His words and ideas are most often a defence of the obvious: people are bad; poems don't need to rhyme; and art is not mere imitation. You always get the feeling when reading him that he's coming at things from first principles. Which is not a bad way to come at things.

19

First principle:

The first point that arises here is grounded in the fact that art in general loves to tarry in the particular. The Understanding hurries, because either it forthwith summarizes variety in a *theory* drawn for generalizations and so evaporates it into reflections and categories, or else it subordinates it into reflections and categories, or else it subordinates it to specific *practical* ends, so that the particular and the individual are not given their full rights. To cling to what, given this position, can only have a relative value, seems therefore to the Understanding to be useless and wearisome. But, in a poetic treatment and formulation, every part, every feature must be interesting and living on its own account, and therefore poetry takes pleasure in lingering over what is individual, describes it with love, and treats it as a whole in itself. Consequently, however great the interest and the subject may be which poetry makes the centre of a work of art, poetry nevertheless articulates it in detail, just as in the human organism each limb, each finger is most delicately rounded off into a whole, and in real life, in short, every particular existent is enclosed into a world of its own. The advance of poetry is therefore slower than the judgements and syllogisms of the Understanding to which what is important, whether in its theorizing or in its practical aims and intentions, is above all the end result, while it is less concerned with the long route by which it reaches it.

G.W.F. HEGEL, *Lectures on Fine Art* (1835), tr. T.M. Knox

The way of the Understanding, Hegel observes, is by reflection and through abstraction. The Understanding tends, especially as it finds its form in philosophy, to present the world in terms of 'categories' and then 'ends'.

'Art in general', on the other hand, and poetry especially, tends otherwise. It 'loves to tarry in the particular'.

Art, that is – forgive us that 'that is' – *expresses* itself throu.
particulars which, in the best poetry, never cease to be particular.

(Which should make us, in passing, be more than a little suspi-
cious of the simile. Or at least, of the simile in general; the simile in
principle.)

What a thing is most like, in poetry, is itself. Poetry does its thinking
in details.

There are many sorts of the particular. Let us tarry in the
particular:

wever minute the employment may appear, of
halysing lines into syllables, and whatever ridicule may
be incurred by a solemn deliberation upon accents and
pauses, it is certain, that without this petty knowledge no
man can be a poet; and that from the proper disposition
of single sounds results that harmony that adds force to
reason, and gives grace to sublimity; that shackles
attention, and governs passions.

SAMUEL JOHNSON, *Rambler*, No. 88 (19 January 1751)

Johnson's 'petty knowledge' here is one sort of particular. As
anyone who has ever studied anything, or fixed anything, or loved
anything will know, petty knowledge is indispensable. Indeed, the
pettier the better.

For the syllable, and its virtues, see also No. 118.

21

Here is another sort of the particular:

I believe in the increasing of life: whatever
Leads to the seeing of small trifles...
Real, beautiful, is good; and an act never
Is worthier than in freeing spirit that stifles
Under ingratitude's weight: nor is anything done
Wiselier than the moving or breaking to sight
Of a thing hidden under by custom; revealed,
Fulfilled, used (sound-fashioned) any way out to delight:

Trefoil...hedge sparrow...the stars on the edge at night.

IVOR GURNEY, 'The Escape' (*c*.1920–22)

Compare and contrast: 'I believe in God the Father Almighty, Maker of heaven and earth: and in Jesus Christ his only Son our Lord, who was conceived by the Holy Ghost, born of the Virgin Mary, suffered under Pontius Pilate, was crucified, dead, and buried, He descended into hell,' et cetera, et cetera.

Ivor Gurney's poem is a creed, a mini- or mimic *Symbolum Apostolorum* (Apostolic Creed), a public statement of faith by a poet intent upon establishing some kind of basis for his own spiritual life.

Gurney has his trinity, his particulars ('Trefoil...hedge sparrow ...the stars on the edge of night'), he states his precepts and his expectations ('revealed, / Fulfilled, used'), and he hints at his own communion ('breaking to sight').

As doctrines go, it's not bad: it lacks perhaps the narrative thrust of the Apostolic Creed, and the poetic flourishes of the Nicene Creed ('We believe in one God, the Father, the Almighty, maker of heaven and earth, of all that is, seen and unseen'), and the punchy quicunqueing of the Athanasian Creed ('Quicunque vult salvus esse'). But at least it's simple and agreeable.

In another poem, 'What I Will Pay', Gurney goes so far as to provide his own outline for discipleship:

> What I will pay to my God is that I will not sleep between sheets,

> Neither take rest unwanted, but work till the first small
> bird fleets
> Past my window

As a guide to the spiritual life, Gurney's methods are both ambitious and rather appealing.

Unfortunately, they also sent him mad.

22

One more sort of the particular, by way of example:

Light   clarity   avocado salad in the morning
after all the terrible things I do how amazing it is
to find forgiveness and love, not even forgiveness
since what is done is done and forgiveness isn't love
and love is love nothing can ever go wrong
though things can get irritating boring and dispensable
(in the imagination) but not really for love
though a block away you feel distant the mere presence
changes everything like a chemical dropped on a paper
and all thoughts disappear in a strange quiet excitement
I am sure of nothing but this, intensified by breathing

FRANK O'HARA, 'Poem' (1959)

This is one of those poems, for Frank O'Hara, in which everything came together.

It is also, one might suggest, with the right degree of lightness and deadly seriousness, a poem in which O'Hara re-writes 1 Corinthians 13.

A treatise on love, 1 Corinthians 13 is also, in the strict sense of the term, a treatise on enthusiasm. 'Though,' Paul writes, 'I speak with the tongues of men and of angels, and have not charity [by which, as modern translators understand it, he means love], I am become *as* sounding brass, or a tinkling cymbal.' And though, he goes on, 'I have the gift of prophecy and understand all mysteries, and all knowledge; and though I have all faith; so that I could remove mountains, and have not charity, I am nothing.' Love 'suffereth long [...] seeketh not her own [...] rejoiceth not in iniquity, but rejoiceth in the truth'. Love 'beareth all things, believeth all things, hopeth all things, endureth all things'.

Our claim that O'Hara re-writes Corinthians can only be a speculation, of course, but can one not perhaps hear Paul coming through here, not only in the comic triad, the petty detail, with which the poem opens, but also in the poem's rhetorical arrangement, in its repetitions and its diction?

since what is done is done and forgiveness isn't love
and love is love nothing can ever go wrong

This is unmistakably O'Hara, but these lines have a sonority and an insistence that comes from elsewhere: O'Hara doesn't, typically, repeat for effect like that; his diction tending rather to alter as rapidly as it presses on. In this, and in the sentiment of forgiveness, there is – perhaps – a deliberate echoing of Paul.

Our other claim, that this is one of those O'Hara poems in which everything comes together, in which he manages, in one brief utterance, to communicate all that mattered to him, is, it turns out, less difficult to prove.

In its basic mechanism, in its account of its own composition, the poem is an act of enthusiasm. Something overwhelming happens – here it is the presence of Vincent, O'Hara's lover, acting on his sensibility like a chemical reaction – from which follows a mood, 'a strange quiet excitement', out of which emerges the possibility of intimate speech. Thus that triad at the beginning is comic, but it is also in earnest.

'Art in general loves to tarry in the particular' (No. 19).

23

Yet there is danger of confusing personal and poetic studies; and there is the fault of writing the personal as if it were poetic.

W.K. WIMSATT (with MONROE C. BEARDSLEY), *The Verbal Icon* (1954)

Quite right.

The particular is not necessarily (in case you have mistaken our mentioning in our discussion of Frank O'Hara's poem a moment ago the pertinent fact of his being in love with someone called Vincent, which is pertinent, but merely a fact) the personal. Though it can be the personal.

Quite right.

24

Poetry is not a turning loose of emotion, but an escape from emotion; it is not the expression of personality, but an escape from personality. But, of course, only those who have personality and emotions know what it means to want to escape from these things.

T.S. ELIOT, 'Tradition and the Individual Talent' (1919)

Again, quite right; Eliot is quite right: it is the poem we are to be interested in. The poet is a distraction.

But Eliot is also wrong, quite wrong: 'only those who have personality and emotions'? '*Only those* who have personality and emotions?' *Only*?

Is this some sort of a joke? Is T.S. Eliot being funny? How many people do you know who *do not* possess personality and emotions?

In fact, does Eliot not precisely indulge himself here? Does he not – it is surely not a mistake to think so – bring his own 'personality and emotions' to the fore? Or the 'personality and emotions' of '*those*' like him; 'personality and emotions' that – how can we not think so – he proposes as superior?

Eliot is right that a poem 'is not a turning loose of emotion', and he is probably right – though you will need to read the whole essay to check – about 'Tradition'. Where he is wrong, here and elsewhere, is about those '*those*'.

25 Au soleil sur mon lit après l'eau
Au soleil et au reflet énorme du soleil sur la mer,
Sous ma fenêtre
Et aux reflets et aux reflets des reflets
Du soleil et des soleils sur la mer
Dans les glaces,
Après le bain, le café, les idées,
Nu au soleil sur mon lit tout illuminé
    Nu, seul, fou,
      Moi!

In the sun on my bed after swimming –
In the sun and in the vast reflection of the sun on the sea,
    Under my window
And in the reflections and the reflections of the reflections
Of the sun and the suns on the sea
    In the mirrors,
After the swim, the coffee, the ideas,
    Naked in the sun on my light-flooded bed
      Naked – alone – mad –
        Me!

PAUL VALÉRY, 'Au Soleil' (1941), tr. Stephen Romer

Valéry presents an option.

And the option is neither working nor shopping.

It is, after the repetitions, and the repetitions, and the repetitions, a mood of composition. Self-composition. Through the articulation of the poem he has arrived at 'Me!'

An escape (see Eliot, previously) can be a return.

See also the following poem by John Keats.

26

There was a naughty boy,
And a naughty boy was he.
He ran away to Scotland,
The people for to see.
Then he found
That the ground
Was as hard,
That a yard
Was as long,
That a song
Was as merry,
That a cherry
Was as red,
That lead
Was as weighty,
That four-score
Was as eighty,
And a door
Was as wooden
As in England.
So he stood in his shoes,
And he wondered,
He wondered,
He stood in his shoes
And he wondered.

JOHN KEATS, from 'A Song About Myself' (1818)

This, if you like, is our stance.

There is no escaping to Scotland. (See *The Thirty-Nine Steps* by John Buchan.)

(See also the previous poem by Paul Valéry.)

27 Prayer the Churches banquet, Angels age,
    God's breath in man returning to his birth,
    The soul in paraphrase, heart in pilgrimage,
The Christian plummet sounding heav'n and earth;
Engine against th' Almightie, sinners towre,
    Reversed thunder, Christ-side-piercing spear,
    The six-daies world transposing in an houre,
A kind of tune, which all things heare and fear;
Softnesse, and peace, and joy, and love, and blisse,
    Exalted Manna, gladnesse of the best,
    Heaven in ordinarie, man well drest,
The milkie way, the bird of Paradise,
    Church-bels beyond the starres heard, the soul's bloud,
    The land of spices; something understood.

GEORGE HERBERT, 'Prayer' (1633)

The question is: what is prayer?

Unable to answer his own question, Herbert, instead, stands in his shoes and wonders. And as he wonders he articulates what is not known. 'Prayer', the poem suggests, can be identified with all that it itemizes, all the particulars that fill out its form. But it is more than each of them; and more than all of them. And in that sense of 'Prayer' being *more* is 'something understood'.

A 'plummet' is a plumb line. Here it sounds heaven and earth.

'Art in general,' let us state once more, for the record, 'loves to tarry in the particular' (No. 19).

Middles

28 Two statements are made as if they are connected, and the reader is forced to consider their relations for himself. The reasons why these facts should have been selected for a poem is left for him to invent; he will invent a variety of reasons and order them in his mind. This, I think, is the essential fact about the poetical use of language.

WILLIAM EMPSON, *Seven Types of Ambiguity* (1930)

William Empson was one of the greatest critics of the 20th century. Which is to say, William Empson was one of the greatest readers of the 20th century. Which is to say – if we take him at his word here – William Empson was a great *inventor*. In *Seven Types of Ambiguity* Empson invented – found, discovered, fabricated, created – seven types of ambiguity, and thus invented himself as a critic.

(Seven types? you might ask. Only seven? Or, as many as seven? The number of days of creation? The days of the week? The ages of man? The number of dwarves? The seven league boots? The hills of Rome? The wonders of the world? The deadly sins? And the virtues? The sacraments? The notes in a scale? The number of habits of highly effective people, according to Stephen R. Covey?)

The poet invents. But the reader invents also.

I would not be hurried by any love of system, by any exaggeration of instincts, to underrate the Book. We all know, that as the human body can be nourished on any food, though it were boiled grass and the broth of shoes, so the human mind can be fed by any knowledge. And great and heroic men have existed, who had almost no other information than by the printed page. I only would say, that it needs a strong head to bear that diet. One must be an inventor to read well. As the proverb says, "He that would bring home the wealth of the Indies, must carry out the wealth of the Indies." There is then creative reading as well as creative writing. When the mind is braced by labour and invention, the page of whatever book we read becomes luminous with manifold allusion. Every sentence is doubly significant, and the sense of our author is as broad as the world.

RALPH WALDO EMERSON, 'The American Scholar' (1837)

It's a crucial statement – 'There is then creative reading as well as creative writing' – a statement more crucial, now, than Emerson could possibly have imagined. Because of course there is now creative writing. Or, rather, Creative Writing (but not, as far as we are aware, Creative Reading).

We recommend, with Emerson, that the mind be 'braced by labour and invention'. It is also greatly to be desired that 'the page of whatever book we read becomes luminous with manifold allusion'. Between writer and reader there has to be a pact.

The pact says that each must make an offering. In writing and reading there is an exchange of gifts. (We shall return, again – and again – to gifts.)

30   **Here is a gift, an example of William Empson's essential fact about the poetical use of language:**

Sur chaque ardoise
           qui glissait du toit
               on
           avait écrit
               un poème

La gouttière est bordée de diamants
               les oiseaux les boivent

On every slate
           sliding from the roof
              someone
              had written
                  a poem

The gutter is rimmed with diamonds
               the birds drink them

PIERRE REVERDY, from *Les Ardoises du Toit* (1918), tr. Patricia Terry

'The gutter is rimmed with diamonds / the birds drink them'.

e simplest rudiment of mystical experience would
em to be that deepened sense of the significance of a
axim or formula which occasionally sweeps over one.
've heard that said all my life,' we exclaim, 'but I never
ealized its full meaning until now.' 'When a fellow-
monk,' said Luther, 'one day repeated the words of the
Creed: "I believe in the forgiveness of sins", I saw the
Scripture in an entirely new light; and straightaway I felt
as if I were born anew. It was as if I had found the door of
paradise thrown wide open.' This sense of deeper signifi-
cance is not confined to rational propositions. Single
words, and conjunctions of words, effects of light on land
and sea, odours and musical sounds, all bring it when
the mind is tuned aright. Most of us can remember the
strangely moving power of passages in certain poems read
when we were young, irrational doorways as they were
through which the mystery of fact, the wildness and the
pang of life, stole into our hearts and thrilled them. The
words have now perhaps become mere polished surfaces
for us; but lyric poetry and music are alive and significant
only in proportion as they fetch these vague vistas of a
life continuous with our own, beckoning and inviting,
yet ever eluding our pursuit. We are alive or dead to the
eternal inner message of the arts according as we have
kept or lost this mystical susceptibility.

WILLIAM JAMES, *The Varieties of Religious Experience* (1902)

**The point here, the phrase, for us, is not 'mystical susceptibility';
we are not, personally, particularly susceptible to 'mystical
susceptibility'.**

**The point here, the phrase, for us, is the rather less vague 'vague
vistas of a life continuous with our own'.**

**Here, we know what James means. We know what he means
when he says, 'I never realized its full meaning until now.' Only
we never *realized* its full meaning until now. It's what Heidegger
means, perhaps, when he speaks of the 'shudder'. Or what Charles
Lamb means, in another context, when he writes of the 'ticklish'.
It's that moment, to refer back to George Herbert (No. 27),
when a poem plummets, and when, in that plummeting, some-
thing is understood.**

Or it's like when Eliot says, in 'East Coker' (*Four Quartets*), that 'In my beginning is my end', and then says later, modifying his formulation, that 'In my end is my beginning' (which was the motto of Mary Queen of Scots), which modulation causes the poem to reverberate with all manner of beginnings and ends; which reverberation, as the poem practices its allusions – *Four Quartets*, of all poems, is 'luminous with manifold allusion' (No. 29) – brings into view both the poem's beginnings, and its end.

Or it's what Derrida means when he speaks of the way words 'tremble', the moments when the differing meanings and possibilities of a word are released.

And James's point is that we should not dismiss such moments. And nor should we grow out of them. And as he says, and as we've been trying to say, you can come across it in a single word.

Like 'beginning'.

Or 'end'.

Or, if we might say so, 'touch':

32

A slumber did my spirit seal;
   I had no human fears:
She seemed a thing that could not feel
   The touch of earthly years.

No motion has she now, no force;
   She neither hears nor sees;
Rolled round in earth's diurnal course,
   With rocks, and stones, and trees.

WILLIAM WORDSWORTH, 'A slumber did my spirit seal'

touch v. 1 come into or be in contact with. 2 harm or interfere with. 3 have an effect on. 4 produce feelings of gratitude or sympathy. 5 *informal* reach. 6 [as adj. touched] *informal* slightly mad. 7 lightly mark in details with a brush or pencil.

Who 'Lucy' was is not certain. That Wordsworth was 'touched' by her is clear. 'Touch' – the 'touch' of her – is what, in his grief, surely, he most misses. It is there that the poem is, as James said, 'beckoning and inviting' – if, by definition, 'eluding our pursuit'.

33 She hears, upon that water without sound,
A voice that cries, "The tomb in Palestine
Is not the porch of spirits lingering.
It is the grave of Jesus, where he lay."
We live in an old chaos of the sun,
Or old dependency of day and night,
Or island solitude, unsponsored, free,
Of that wide water, inescapable.
Deer walk upon our mountains, and the quail
Whistle about us their spontaneous cries;
Sweet berries ripen in the wilderness;
And, in the isolation of the sky,
At evening, casual flocks of pigeons make
Ambiguous undulations as they sink,
Downward to darkness, on extended wings.

WALLACE STEVENS, from 'Sunday Morning' (1923)

And so, inevitably, via Wordsworth, we get to the heart of the matter.

The heart of the matter, at any rate, as far as the Modernist American poet Wallace Stevens understands it.

Jesus is dead. 'We live in an old chaos of the sun'. Where, the poem, wonders, is the consolation to be found?

What it looks like, what the poem allows it to seem like, is that the consolation is to be found in nature, where – beautiful lines – 'Sweet berries ripen in the wilderness; / And, in the isolation of the sky / At evening, casual flocks of pigeons make / Ambiguous undulations as they sink'.

But this is not what the poem says. The consolation, here, is not – as in Wordsworth – to be found in nature, but in the beauty of the language which makes our idea of nature possible. Maybe sweet berries *do* ripen in the wilderness. It's not the fact, though, but the saying of the fact that makes the line lovely. It's the way also, in the next line, the word 'And' is emphasized – to give the line weight, to give the reader pause. Which has nothing to do with nature, and everything to do with the fact that, at the beginning of this line of iambic pentameter, the stress falls on the first (not the second) syllable.

Or think about those deer. Do they really 'walk upon our mountains'? And do 'the quail' really 'whistle about *us* their spontaneous cries'? And what does it mean to speak of the spontaneous cry of the quail any way? And if you hadn't got the point already – and Stevens does really want us to get the point – when did you ever see a pigeon ambiguously undulate?

And so here is the point: faced with the God-less chaos of a meaningless universe, the only consolation the poem has to offer is language's capacity to give nature meaning. The beauty of the poem is the poem's beauty. 'Poetry,' as Stevens says in another poem, is the 'supreme fiction'.

Or to put this another way: the world isn't meaningful; words are meaningful.

The question is – and here you have to keep your eye on the deer – which words?

34 The pure products of America
go crazy—
mountain folk from Kentucky

or the ribbed north end of
Jersey
with its isolate lakes and

valleys, its deaf-mutes, thieves
old names
and promiscuity between

devil-may-care men who have taken
to railroading
out of sheer lust of adventure—

and young slatterns, bathed
in filth
from Monday to Saturday

to be tricked out that night
with gauds
from imaginations which have no

peasant traditions to give them
character
but flutter and flaunt

sheer rags—succumbing without
emotion
save numbed terror

under some hedge of choke-cherry
or viburnum—
which they cannot express—

Unless it be that marriage
perhaps
with a dash of Indian blood

will throw up a girl so desolate
so hemmed round
with disease or murder

that she'll be rescued by an
agent—
reared by the state and

sent out at fifteen to work in
some hard-pressed
house in the suburbs—

some doctor's family, some Elsie—
voluptuous water
expressing with broken

brain the truth about us—
her great
ungainly hips and flopping breasts

addressed to cheap
jewelry
and rich young men with fine eyes

as if the earth under our feet
were
an excrement of some sky

and we degraded prisoners
destined
to hunger until we eat filth

while the imagination strains
after deer
going by fields of goldenrod in

the stifling heat of September
somehow
it seems to destroy us

It is only in isolate flecks that
something
is given off

No one
to witness
and adjust, no one to drive the car

WILLIAM CARLOS WILLIAMS, 'To Elsie' (1923)

This is a great poem. What would you give to have written that poem? As much as Ben Jonson would have given to have written Southwell's 'The Burning Babe' (No. 127)?

About the deer, though. Do *deer* walk on *our* mountains? William Carlos Williams thinks not. The poetic imagination, he suggests, 'strains after deer', 'as if the earth under our feet / were / an excrement of some sky'.

The question for Williams, who admired Stevens and disagreed with him, is what the poem should consist of: whether its particulars should be the already worked over phrases of old poems, or the changing particulars of a new world.

The world in which he finds himself, the America, here, of the 1920s, was a world, as he saw it, without a tradition, a world with no centre but only margins.

In his poetry Williams set out to fill the gap. He set out to make a modern tradition. He writes of 'railroading' men and 'slatterns'. These, not the deer, he suggests, are the 'pure products of America'.

Anyway, our question was, which words? The diction of poets, or the diction of people? 'Fields of goldenrod', or as the poem says, 'some Elsie'?

'Elsie', in this case anyway, is the key. She is the figure in the poem who brings the whole set of crazy images together. She is part Native American. She is 'reared by the state'. She works for some doctor's family in the suburbs. In her mix of attributes and experiences she holds everything together. The modern tradition, the poem asserts, originates in the broken home. 'To Elsie', in its craving after attachment, is a dysfunctional love poem.

But just stop for a moment. Read the poem again. Read it out loud. Read it quickly. The poem is quick. It is quick because it has to keep up.

It has to keep up because there is 'no one to drive the car'.

Except, of course, for the poet. Keeping an eye, naturally, on those deer:

35 Traveling through the dark I found a deer
dead on the edge of the Wilson River road.
It is usually best to roll them into the canyon:
that road is narrow; to swerve might make more dead.

By glow of the tail-light I stumbled back of the car
and stood by the heap, a doe, a recent killing;
she had stiffened already, almost cold.
I dragged her off; she was large in the belly.

My fingers touching her side brought me the reason—
her side was warm; her fawn lay there waiting,
alive, still, never to be born.
Beside that mountain road I hesitated.

The car aimed ahead its lowered parking lights;
under the hood purred the steady engine.
I stood in the glare of the warm exhaust turning red;
around our group I could hear the wilderness listen.

I thought hard for us all—my only swerving—,
then pushed her over the edge into the river.

WILLIAM STAFFORD, 'Traveling Through The Dark' (1962)

In William Stafford's poem not only is the deer dead, there's nothing – so the speaker decides – to be done for the fawn.

And again, there is no one behind the wheel: the narrator has got out of the car.

But the engine is still purring, 'the warm exhaust turning red'.

36

ROASTBEEF; MUTTON; BREAKFAST; SUGAR;
CRANBERRIES; MILK; EGGS; APPLE; TAILS; LUNCH;
CUPS; RHUBARB; SINGLE FISH; CAKE; CUSTARD;
POTATOES; ASPARAGUS; BUTTER; END OF SUMMER;
SAUSAGES; CELERY; VEAL; VEGETABLE; COOKING;
CHICKEN; PASTRY; CREAM; CUCUMBER; DINNER;
DINING; EATING; SALAD; SAUCE; SALMON;
ORANGE; COCOA; AND CLEAR SOUP AND ORANGES
AND OATMEAL; SALAD DRESSING AND AN
ARTICHOKE; A CENTRE IN A TABLE.

GERTRUDE STEIN, 'Food', from *Tender Buttons* (1914)

No actual food here, of course, only words: 'ASPARAGUS';
'SAUSAGES'.

But these are words different enough from one another to be
savoured. Words, one might think, for the tongue, not for the
table.

But then as Stevens said, more than once: 'I repeat that [the poet's]
role is to help people live their lives. He has had immensely to
do with giving life whatever savor it possesses. He has had to do
with whatever the imagination and senses have made of
the world.'

And the way the poet does this, as Stevens saw it – the way the
poet 'savors' life – is very largely through the 'music' of words.
There, in the sounds of the words, is the quality of distinction that
makes 'savoring' possible: 'ASPARAGUS'; 'SAUSAGES'; 'CELERY';
and 'VEAL'.

37

The future of poetry is immense, because in poetry, where it is worthy of its high destinies, our race, as time goes on, will find an ever surer and surer stay. [...] More and more mankind will discover that we have to turn to poetry to interpret life for us, to console us, to sustain us.

MATTHEW ARNOLD, 'The Study of Poetry' (1880)

To savour life, as Stevens has it, or to sustain us, as Matthew Arnold has it?

38 Besides, men who read from religious or moral inclinations, even when the subject is of a kind of which they approve, are beset with misconceptions and mistakes peculiar to themselves. Attaching so much importance to the truths which interest them, they are prone to overrate the authors by whom these truths are expressed and enforced. They come prepared to impart so much passion to the poet's language, that they remain unconscious, how little, in fact, they receive from it.

WILLIAM WORDSWORTH, Essay Supplementary to the Preface, *Lyrical Ballads* (1815)

The question is, does the poet give us enough? The question is, does Stein give us enough? The question is, when is a poem enough? When, the question is, does a savour become sustaining?

39 My future will not copy fair my past
On any leaf but Heaven's. Be fully done,
Supernal Will! I would not fain be one
Who, satisfying thirst and breaking fast
Upon the fullness of the heart, at last
Says no grace after meat. My wine has run
Indeed out of my cup, and there is none
To gather up the bread of my repast
Scattered and trampled, – yet I find some good
In earth's green herbs, and streams that bubble up
Clear from the darkling ground, – content until
I sit with angels before better food.
Dear Christ! when Thy new vintage fills my cup,
This hand shall shake no more, nor that wine spill.

ELIZABETH BARRETT BROWNING, 'Past and Future' (1856)

The word, unquestionably, is 'spill'. For Elizabeth Barrett Browning it signifies waste. It rhymes, in the poem, with 'Supernal Will', and 'until', and 'fill'. To spill Christ's wine would be to display ingratitude; as if not saying grace after eating one's meat.

The commandment, the poem perhaps suggests, is 'Thou shalt not spill'.

40 We that have done and thought,
That have thought and done,
Must ramble, and thin out
Like milk spilt on a stone.

W.B. YEATS, 'Spilt Milk' (1933)

Yeats, crying over spilt milk.

'We that have done and thought, / That have thought and done'?

Yeats reminds us of T.S. Eliot. We can never tell if he's joking: is there anyone, any man, woman or child, who hasn't done and thought, and thought and done? Maybe 'We' is everyone. Maybe not. Our problem is, we can't tell.

The problem here is the pronoun, the invidious 'We'. Is that a discriminating 'We' as in 'Eliot's 'those' (No. 24), or something more universal? Perhaps in this case it's the latter – the problem, after all, is ageing. At some point we must all, if we get that far, 'ramble, and thin out'. Which would make the spilt milk not a cause of private regret, but a reason for general human lamentation: the milk in question being what, in part, humanizes us, the fluid which makes 'us', if we might say so, mammalian.

(A mammal, the *OED* explains, is: 'An animal of the vertebrate class Mammalia, the members of which are characterized by having mammary glands that secrete milk to feed the young.')

Compare and contrast the next poem, by Paul Celan.

The critic George Steiner has remarked that: 'The quality of aloneness in Celan is pitiless.' There is a quality, one might say, in Yeats that is piti*ful*.

41

Schwarze Milch der Frühe wir trinken sie abends
wir trinken sie mittags und morgens wir trinken sie
    nachts
wir trinken und trinken
wir schaufeln ein Grab in den Lüften da liegt man nicht
    eng
Ein Mann wohnt im Haus der spielt mit den Schlangen
    der schreibt
der schreibt wenn es dunkelt nach Deutschland dein
    goldenes Haar Margarete
er schreibt es und tritt vor das Haus und es blitzen die
    Sterne er pfeift seine Rüden herbei
er pfeift seine Juden hervor läßt schaufeln ein Grab in der
    Erde
er befiehlt uns spielt auf nun zum Tanz

Schwarze Milch der Frühe wir trinken dich nachts
wir trinken dich morgens und mittags wir trinken dich
    abends
wir trinken und trinken
Ein Mann wohnt im Haus der spielt mit den Schlangen
    der schreibt
der schreibt wenn es dunkelt nach Deutschland dein
    goldenes Haar Margarete
Dein aschenes Haar Sulamith wir schaufeln ein Grab in
    den Lüften da liegt man nicht eng

Er ruft stecht tiefer ins Erdreich ihr einen ihr andern
    singet und spielt
er greift nach dem Eisen im Gurt er schwingts seine
    Augen sind blau
stecht tiefer die Spaten ihr einen ihr andern spielt wieter
    zum Tanz auf

Schwarze Milch der Frühe wir trinken dich nachts
wir trinken dich mittags und morgens wir trinken dich
    abends
wir trinken und trinken
ein Mann wohnt im Haus dein goldenes Haar Margarete
dein aschenes Haar Sulamith er spielt mit den Schlangen

Er ruft spielt süßer den Tod der Tod ist ein Meister aus
     Deutschland
er ruft streicht dunkler die Geigen dann steigt ihr als
     Rauch in die Luft
dann habt ihr ein Grab in den Wolken da liegt man nicht eng

Schwarze Milch der Frühe wir trinken dich nachts
wir trinken dich mittags der Tod ist ein Meister aus
     Deutschland
wir trinken dich abends und morgens wir trinken und
     trinken
der Tod ist ein Meister aus Deutschland sein Auge ist blau
er trifft dich mit bleierner Kugel er trifft dich genau
ein Mann wohnt im Haus dein goldenes Haar Margarete
er hetzt seine Rüden auf uns er schenkt uns ein Grab in
     der Luft
er spielt mit den Schlangen und träumet der Tod ist ein
     Meister aus Deutschland

dein goldenes Haar Margarete
dein aschenes Haar Sulamith

Black milk of daybreak we drink it at sundown
we drink it at noon in the morning we drink it at night
we drink and we drink it
we dig a grave in the breezes there one lies unconfined
A man lives in the house he plays with the serpents he
     writes
he writes when dusk falls to Germany your golden hair
     Margarete
he writes it and steps out of doors and the stars are
     flashing he whistles his pack out
he whistles his Jews out in earth has them dig for a grave
he commands us strike up for the dance

Black milk of daybreak we drink you at night
we drink in the morning at noon we drink you at
     sundown
we drink and we drink you
A man lives in the house he plays with the serpents he
     writes

he writes when dusk falls to Germany your golden hair
    Margarete
your ashen hair Shulamith we dig a grave in the breezes
    there one lies unconfined

He calls out jab deeper into the earth you lot you others
    sing now and play
he grabs at the iron in his belt he waves it his eyes are blue
jab deeper you lot with your spades you others play on
    for the dance

Black milk of daybreak we drink you at night
we drink you at noon in the morning we drink you at
    sundown
we drink and we drink you
a man lives in the house your golden hair Margarete
your ashen hair Shulamith he plays with the serpents

He calls out more sweetly play death death is a master
    from Germany
he calls out more darkly now stroke your strings then as
    smoke you will rise into air
then a grave you will have in the clouds there one lies
    unconfined

Black milk of daybreak we drink you at night
we drink you at noon death is a master from Germany
we drink you at sundown and in the morning we drink
    and we drink you
death is a master from Germany his eyes are blue
he strikes you with leaden bullets his aim is true
a man lives in the house your golden hair Margarete
he sets his pack onto us he grants us a grave in the air
plays with the serpents and daydreams death is a master
    from Germany

your golden hair Margarete
your ashen hair Shulamith

PAUL CELAN, 'Todesfuge' (1952), tr. Michael Hamburger

Schwarze Milch. Black milk.

Black milk?

Black milk.

Even in Celan – that most troubling, puzzling, even at times one might say *illegible* of poets – there is this basic, most pleasing, most shockingly *obvious* of lyric poetry's many devices: oxymoron. And we drink it and drink it. Wir trinken und trinken.

The poem's original title was 'Death Tango' (in German). Celan changed tango to fugue.

A fugue, according to our dictionary, is: 'The most fully developed procedure of imitative counterpoint, in which the theme is stated successively in all voices of the polyphonic texture, tonally established, continuously expanded, opposed, and re-established; also the genre designation for a work employing this procedure.'

See also Heidegger (No. 43).

42 Cell by cell the baby made herself, the cells
Made cells. This is to say
The baby is made largely of milk. Lying in her father's
    arms, the little seed eyes
Moving, trying to see, smiling for us
To see, she will make a household
To her need of these rooms—Sara, little seed,
Little violent, diligent seed. Come let us look at the world
Glittering: this seed will speak,
Max, words! There will be no other words in the world
But those our children speak. What will she make of a
    world
Do you suppose, Max, of which she is made.

GEORGE OPPEN, 'Sara in Her Father's Arms' (1962)

Here, as we approach the middle – or at least a middle of the middle – is another beginning. Or, at least, a counterpoint. An expansion. A re-establishing.

Our word now is not 'spill' or 'spilt', but 'milk'. 'The baby is made largely of milk.' The question, though, is what she will make, where what she can make depends largely on what she is made of. 'What will she make of a world / Do you suppose, Max, of which she is made.'

But what she will make depends also on her words, which is why the poet is so attentive to her. Oppen, writing in the 1960s, understood that words badly used could do terrible harm. In that – in this – he is like Celan. The crucial thing for both poets was to use words with care. Not, as Elizabeth Barrett Browning might have thought also, to 'spill' them, but to use them truthfully, one by one.

43 To be sure, the sculptor uses stone just as the mason uses it, in his own way. But he does not use it up. That happens in a certain way only where the work miscarries. To be sure, the painter also uses pigment, but in such a way that colour is not used up but rather only now comes to shine forth. To be sure, the poet also uses the word – not, however, like ordinary speakers and writers who have to use them up, but rather in such a way that the word only now becomes and remains truly a word.

MARTIN HEIDEGGER, from 'The Origin of the Work of Art' (1936),
Martin Heidegger: Basic Writings, tr. David Farrell Krell

See Paul Celan (No. 41).

Heidegger and Paul Celan; Paul Celan and Heidegger. The Jew and the National Socialist, and the true use of words. And Oppen, a Jew and Communist, citing Heidegger at the beginning of his long poem *Of Being Numerous*.

Celan's parents died in a labour camp. Heidegger was a member of the Nazi party. The two men met in 1967. No one knows what they said at their meeting (although *The Enthusiast* would like to recommend to readers of a philosophical bent or proclivity the book *La Poesie comme experience* by Philippe Lacoue-Labarthe, available in an English translation, *Poetry as Experience*, by Andrea Tarnowski, published in 1999, which offers possibilities; and we would recommend also John Felstiner's biography of Celan; and Heidegger, of course, *Being and Time*; and Celan's poem 'Todtnauberg', which commemorates – or marks, rather – the meeting with Heidegger).

We are particularly mindful, conducting our own enterprise, of the end of Celan's poem 'Nächtlich Geschürzt', or rather, in its English translation by Michael Hamburger, 'Nocturnally Pouting':

A word – you know:
a corpse.

Let us wash it,
let us comb it,
let us turn its eye
towards heaven.

Almost like an eye upon a forehead of a bust that knows it cannot see:

44 The difference between Despair
And Fear—is like the One
Between the instant of a Wreck—
And when the Wreck has been—

The mind is smooth—no Motion—
Contented as the Eye
Upon that forehead of a Bust—
That knows—it cannot see—

EMILY DICKINSON, Poem 305 (*c*.1862)

The difference was Emily Dickinson's subject: the difference between herself and others; the difference between herself and God; the difference between states; between life and death; the difference, as here, between words.

And here she catches it, the difference between 'Despair / And Fear'.

It's the difference, as she says, between 'the instant of a Wreck— / And when the Wreck has been'.

Consider that last phrase. That's the difference. The moment after is final. Fear speaks of what is coming. Despair speaks to what is done.

Great poets, if we might generalize, distinguish between just such instants.

45

We must love one another or die.

W.H. AUDEN, from 'September 1, 1939'

This is the last line of W.H. Auden's poem 'September 1, 1939'. It fails to mark a true difference, to distinguish between instants. It is, in fact, simply wrong, insofar as it is not true. 'We must love one another or die'? No. There is no either/or. We die anyway.

Auden knew it was wrong. He described 'September 1, 1939' as one of the most dishonest poems he'd ever written (and he wrote quite a few dishonest poems). He tried to make it right: he was a good person, always trying to make things right, forever fiddling with his poems. Even once they were published he would seek to revise them, in subsequent editions of his work altering and omitting lines and stanzas that no longer struck him as correct.

Auden's most famous revision was of this very line from 'September 1, 1939' (the title is the date of Hitler's invasion of Poland). The poem was first published in October 1939. By 1945 Auden had changed the 'or' for an 'and' so that the line reads: 'We must love one another and die.'

But this is also wrong. 'We must love one another and die' makes loving seem pointless.

The problem may not in fact lie in the 'or' or the 'and'. The problem may lie in the 'must'.

Auden later omitted the entire stanza in which the line appears.

A poem, naturally, can be wrong. And more than once.

46

What the imagination seizes as beauty must be truth [...].

JOHN KEATS, letter to Benjamin Bailey, 22 November 1817

Or not.

See previous.

47 Every poem starts out as either true or beautiful. Then you try to make the true ones seem beautiful and the beautiful ones true.

PHILIP LARKIN, from *Larkin at Sixty*, ed. Anthony Thwaite (1982)

This seems perhaps closer to the truth of being true, but it has the disadvantage of making poetry sound like Plasticine.

At least, though, Larkin allows for the possibility of errIng:

48 The mere word "freedom" is the only one that still excites me. I deem it capable of indefinitely sustaining the old human fanaticism. It doubtless satisfies my only legitimate aspiration. Among all the many misfortunes to which we are heir, it is only fair to admit that were are allowed the greatest degree of freedom of thought. It is up to us not to misuse it. To reduce the imagination to a state of slavery – even though it would mean the elimination of what is commonly called happiness – is to betray all sense of absolute justice within oneself. Imagination alone offers me some intimation of what *can be*, and this is enough to remove to some slight degree the terrible injunction; enough, too, to allow me to devote myself to it without fear of making a mistake (as though it were possible to make a bigger mistake). Where does it begin to turn bad, and where does the mind's stability cease? For the mind, is the possibility of erring not rather the contingency of good?

ANDRÉ BRETON, 'Manifesto of Surrealism' (1924), tr. Richard Seaver and Helen R. Lane

To err, one might think, is human; to forgive divine. See later (No. 148).

The freedom of the poet, more precisely, is the possibility of erring. In erring begins possibility.

Breton had served as a nurse in World War One, in which technologically advanced conflict he considered he had witnessed the triumph of excessive rationality. Against rationality he posed the imagination: 'Imagination alone offers me some intimation of what *can be*.'

It is the poet's responsibility, Breton considered, to err. Out of that erring new possibilities for human existence would arise.

Except that, of course – and we will come onto this later also, much, much later – freedom is both a blessing and a curse. It is a double-edged sword.

What was it that Whitman sought to export if not freedom? And would Whitman, we wonder, endorse the exporting of freedom now?

As for the 'free' word: does it not become untethered? Are there not perhaps ways in which the word should be held down?

Even so, we must allow poems to make mistakes. Poems *are* mistakes:

49 If you can keep your head when all about you
　　Are losing theirs and blaming it on you,
If you can trust yourself when all men doubt you,
　　But make allowance for their doubting too;
If you can wait and not be tired by waiting,
　　Or being lied about, don't deal in lies,
Or being hated, don't give way to hating,
　　And yet don't look too good, nor talk too wise:

If you can dream—and not make dreams your master;
　　If you can think—and not make thoughts your aim;
If you can meet with Triumph and Disaster
　　And treat those two impostors just the same;
If you can bear to hear the truth you've spoken
　　Twisted by knaves to make a trap for fools,
Or watch the things you give your life to, broken,
　　And stoop and build 'em up with worn-out tools:

If you can make one heap of all your winnings
　　And risk it on one turn of pitch-and-toss,
And lose, and start again at your beginnings
　　And never breathe a word about your loss;
If you can force your heart and nerve and sinew
　　To serve your turn long after they are gone,
And so hold on when there is nothing in you
　　Except the Will which says to them: 'Hold on!'

If you can talk with crowds and keep your virtue,
　　Or walk with Kings—nor lose the common touch,
If neither foes nor loving friends can hurt you,
　　If all men count with you, but none too much;
If you can fill the unforgiving minute
　　With sixty seconds' worth of distance run,
Yours is the Earth and everything that's in it,
　　And—which is more—you'll be a Man, my son!

RUDYARD KIPLING, 'If' (1910)

**This is an exhortation rather than a prescription, an expression of
a deep longing rather than a set of requirements: no man could
stand such proving.**

The only possibility Kipling in fact presents us with is failure.

It's an interesting possibility.

50 Intimacy cannot be expressed discursively.

The swelling to the bursting point, the malice that breaks out with clenched teeth and weeps; the sinking feeling that doesn't know where it comes from or what it's about; the fear that sings its head off in the dark; the white-eyed pallor, the sweet sadness, the rage and the vomiting ... are so many evasions.

What is intimate, in the strong sense, is what has the passion of an absence of individuality, the imperceptible sonority of a river, the empty limpidity of the sky: this is still a negative definition, from which the essential is missing.

These statements have the vague quality of inaccessible distances, but on the other hand articulated definitions substitute the tree for the forest, the distant articulation for that which is articulated.

I will resort to articulation nevertheless.

GEORGES BATAILLE, *Theory of Religion* (1948), tr. Robert Hurley

Herewith, the paradox.

Always the poet resorts to articulation. Yet it is an article of poetic faith that intimacy cannot be expressed discursively.

The latter is surely obvious. Why else would poets keep trying? It is because intimacy evades articulation that poets keep on keeping on.

The *more* intimate statement, in Bataille's view, is the one which conspicuously lacks intimacy, 'the empty limpidity of the sky'. There, at least, the intimacy is consciously missed.

Anything else, he suggests, substitutes 'the tree for the forest', which is, perhaps, to say the simile for the intimacy. Which is perhaps to say, 'My love is like a red, red rose.'

Love is not like a red, red rose – ours isn't anyway – but the claim is that it is. And so the 'rose' (the tree) stands in for love ('the forest').

As a writer, Bataille 'will resort to articulation nevertheless'.

So, more failure. More productive erring.

(Note the 'swelling to bursting point': we shall return later to swelling and bursting.)

51

They sing their dearest songs –
He, she, all of them – yea,
Treble and tenor and bass,
    And one to play;
With the candles mooning each face ...
    Ah, no; the years O!
How the sick leaves reel down in throngs!

They clear the creeping moss –
Elders and juniors – aye,
Making the pathways neat
    And the garden gay;
And they build a shady seat ...
    Ah, no; the years, the years;
See the white storm-birds wing across!

They are blithely breakfasting all –
Men and maidens, yea,
Under the summer tree,
    With a glimpse of the bay,
While pet fowl come to the knee ...
    Ah, no; the years O!
And the rotten rose is ript from the wall.

They change to a high new house,
He, she, all of them – aye,
Clocks and carpets and chairs
    On the lawn all day,
And brightest things that are theirs ...
    Ah, no; the years, the years;
Down their carved names the rain-drop ploughs.

THOMAS HARDY, 'During Wind and Rain' (1914)

Thomas Hardy, resorting to articulation.

This is a poem about time, and it is carefully timed, with its 'Ah's and 'yea's and 'aye's and 'O's, and its little tableaux, and most of all with its shocking final line, and the revelation that these people Hardy is writing about – ah, no – are already dead.

And it's a 'rotten rose', note, in this poem of evasions, that is 'ript from the wall'. The poem, like the rose, is a series of failures to say.

It is a poem full of contrary motions – yea, no.

52 When you imagine trumpet-faced musicians
blowing again inimitable jazz
no art can accuse nor cannonadings hurt,

or coming out of your dreams of dirigibles
again see the unreasonable cripple
throwing his crutch headlong as the headlights

streak down the torn street, as the three hammerers
go One, Two, Three on the stake, triphammer poundings
and not a sign of new worlds to still the heart;

then stare into the lake of sunset as it runs
boiling, over the west past all control
rolling and swamps the heartbeat and repeats
sea beyond sea after unbearable suns;
think: poems fixed this landscape: Blake, Donne, Keats.

MURIEL RUKEYSER, 'Homage to Literature' (1938)

Muriel Rukeyser was not only a poet. She was also a political activist. Witness her injunction: 'When', '*then*', '*think*'.

Her 'Keats' rhymes with 'repeats'. And the word she repeats is 'again'. Again with the 'trumpet-faced musicians'. Again with the 'dreams of dirigibles'.

These images, she says, are not new (she was writing in the 1930s). The question is, when will there be 'a sign of new worlds to still the heart'?

To which the answer is '*think:* poems fixed this landscape'.

Which means, we think, that we may need new poems, new ways of seeing new landscapes. Because the only true homage to literature *is* literature, which is to say, *doing* something.

53

When I find people ridiculing the new arts, or makin[g] fun of the clumsy odd terms that we use in trying to t[alk] of them amongst ourselves; when they laugh at our talking about the "ice-block quality" in Picasso, I think it is only because they do not know what thought is like, and that they are familiar only with argument, gibe and opinion. That is to say, they can only enjoy what they have been brought up to consider enjoyable, or what some essayist has talked about in mellifluous phrases. They think only "the shells of thought" as De Gourmont calls them; the thoughts that have already been thought by others.

Any mind that is worth calling a mind must have needs beyond the existing categories of language, just as a painter must have pigments or shades more numerous than the existing names of the colours.

EZRA POUND, 'Vorticism', in *Gaudier-Brzeska: A Memoir* (1916)

Pound is doing something here, something fine, and we are in entire agreement with him. Almost, and until. Until he reaches 'Any mind that is worth calling a mind'.

What Pound does, and says, famously, is 'Make it New!' (the 'it' being poetry).

Poetry has to be made new because things change; and because ways of expressing become familiar, and the problem with the familiar is that it militates against thought.

The familiar expression, and in particular the familiar poem, is no more than the shell of thought. Real thought, real thinking, requires striving after what is new.

Everybody has to understand this. Modern artists have to understand it. The audience for art has to understand that newness is what the artist is required to create. And it is true – absolutely true – that the modern poet will have 'needs beyond the existing categories of language'.

The problem, however, is that Pound, like Eliot, has a fondness for dividing us all up: 'Any mind that is worth calling a mind must have needs beyond the existing categories of language'; 'Only those who have personality and emotions know what it means to want to escape from these things' (No. 24).

It is good and necessary to Make it New. It is not good merely to 'gibe'. Pound begins by speaking boldly on behalf of the strange, but proceeds quickly to dismiss anything other: 'Any mind that is worth calling a mind'.

'Ridicule' cuts both ways.

54 Me voici devant tous un homme plein de sens
Connaissant la vie et de la mort ce qu'un vivant peut
    connaître
Ayant éprouvé les douleurs et les joies de l'amour
Ayant su quelquefois imposer ses idées
Connaissant plusieurs langages
Ayant pas mal voyagé
Ayant vu la guerre dans l'Artillerie et l'Infanterie
Blessé à la tête trépané sous le chloroforme
Ayant perdu ses meilleurs amis dans l'effroyable lutte
Je sais d'ancien et de nouveau autant qu'un homme seul
    pourrait des deux savoir
Et sans m'inquiéter aujourd'hui de cette guerre
Entre nous et pour nous mes amis
Je juge cette longue querelle de la tradition et de l'invention
        De l'Ordre et de l'Aventure

Vous dont la bouche est faite à l'image de celle de Dieu
Bouche qui est l'ordre même
Soyez indulgents quand vous nous comparez
À ceux qui furent la perfection de l'ordre
Nous qui quêtons partout l'aventure

Nous ne sommes pas vos ennemis
Nous voulons vous donner de vastes et d'étranges domaines
Où le mystère en fleurs s'offre à qui veut le cueillir
Il y a là des feux nouveaux des couleurs jamais vues
Mille phantasmes impondérables
Auxquels il faut donner de la réalité
Nous voulons explorer la bonté contrée énorme où tout
    se tait
Il y a aussi le temps qu'on peut chasser ou faire revenir
Pitié pour nous qui combattons toujours aux frontières

De l'illimité et de l'avenir
Pitié pour nos erreurs pitié pour nos péchés

Voici que vient l'été la saison violente
Et ma jeunesse est morte ainsi que le printemps
Ô Soleil c'est le temps de la Raison ardente
                Et j'attends
Pour la suivre toujours la forme noble et douce

Qu'elle prend afin que je l'aime seulement
Elle vient et m'attire ainsi qu'un fer l'aimant
Elle a l'aspect charmant
D'une adorable rousse

Ses cheveux sont d'or on dirait
Un bel éclair qui durerait
Ou ces flames qui se pavanent
Dans les roses-thé qui se fanent

Mais riez riez de moi
Hommes de partout surtout gens d'ici
Car il y a tant de choses que je n'ose vous dire
Tant de choses que vous ne me laisserriez pas dire
Ayez pitié de moi

Here I am before you all a man of good sense
Knowing life and as much as the living can know of death
Having been through the pains and joys of love
And having managed now and again to make people
respect my ideas
Knowing several languages
Having travelled widely
Having seen war with the Artillery and the Infantry
And having been wounded in the head and trepanned
under chloroform
Having lost my best friends in the terrible struggle
I know both old and new as much as one man can ever
hope to
And without worrying for the moment about this war
Between ourselves my friends and for ourselves
I shall judge this long quarrel between tradition and invention
Between Order and Adventure

You whose mouth is made in the image of God's
Mouth that is order itself
Be indulgent when you compare us
To those who were the perfection of order
Us who seek everywhere for adventure

We are not your enemies
We want to give you vast and strange worlds
Where flowering mystery yields to whoever wants to pick it
Where there are new fires colours never seen before
A thousand weightless phantoms
That must be made real
We want to explore kindness that vast countrywhere all is
     silent
And then there is time that can be banished or recalled
Pity us who are always fighting on the frontiers
Of infinity and the future
Pity our mistakes pity our sins

Summer's on the way season of violence
And like the Spring my youth is dead
Now O sun it is the time of ardent reason
               And I intend
To follow for ever the sweet and noble form
She's taken on so I'll love her and no one else
Here she comes drawing me after her as a magnet draws iron
               And she is lovely
               And has red hair

Her hair is gold it's like
A lightning flash that doesn't stop
Or the flames that go on glowing
In a fading rose

But laugh laugh at me
Men everywhere especially people here
For there are so many things I'm afraid to tell you
So many things you'd never let me tell you
Have pity on me

GUILLAUME APOLLINAIRE, 'La jolie rousse' (1918), tr. Robert
Chandler

Yankee Pound demands our assent.

Neo-Surrealist Apollinaire appeals for our indulgence.

**Both poets provoke laughter. Pound resents it. Apollinaire
invites it.**

Pound tells us what we ought to like. Apollinaire sets out before us what he has to offer.

As for the 'long quarrel between tradition and invention', see Empson (No. 28).

As for 'Us who seek everywhere for adventure', see Milton (No. 4) and Tennyson (No. 147).

55

Oh, to be in England
Now that April's there,
And whoever wakes in England
Sees, some morning, unaware,
That the lowest boughs and the brushwood sheaf
Round the elm-tree bole are in tiny leaf,
While the chaffinch sings on the orchard bough
In England – now!

ROBERT BROWNING, from 'Home-Thoughts, from Abroad' (1845)

English Browning, yearning.

56

Quinquireme of Nineveh from distant Ophir
Rowing home to haven in sunny Palestine,
    With a cargo of ivory
    And apes and peacocks,
Sandalwood, cedarwood, and sweet white wine.

Stately Spanish galleon coming from the Isthmus,
Dipping through the Tropics by the palm-green shores,
    With a cargo of diamonds,
    Emeralds, amethysts,
Topazes, and cinnamon, and gold moidores.

Dirty British coaster with a salt-caked smoke stack
Butting through the Channel in the mad March days,
    With a cargo of Tyne coal,
    Road-rail, pig-lead,
Firewood, ironware, and cheap tin trays.

JOHN MASEFIELD, 'Cargoes' (1910)

This is a poem expressing shame, disappointment and disgust. Note that the British coaster is first and foremost 'Dirty': it is unclean; repugnant.

Of course, a lot of poems express shame, disappointment and disgust: shame, disappointment and disgust are easy and popular emotions. Anyone can feel shame, disappointment and disgust.

Masefield is disgusted in particular by industrialization and its products. The feelings of many people of many ages were and are similar on this matter to Masefield's, and Masefield was indeed at one time, and not surprisingly, an enormously popular poet. He was Poet Laureate for 37 years.

And yet no one reads him now at all. He wrote hundreds of books: novels, plays, poetry, biography, autobiography, literary criticism. And now the only piece of work of his that anyone knows is 'Cargoes', a poem freighted with its own disgust.

Perhaps this is because disgust, as expressed in this poem, and familiar to us all whatever its apparent association or means of expression, reveals itself eventually as a disgust of humanity.

57

An old, mad, blind, despised, and dying king, –
Princes, the dregs of their dull race, who flow
Through public scorn, – mud from a muddy spring, –
Rulers who neither see, nor feel, nor know,
But leech-like to their fainting country cling,
Till they drop, blind in blood, without a blow, –
A people starved and stabbed in the untilled field, –
An army, which liberticide and prey
Makes as a two-edged sword to all who wield, –
Golden and sanguine laws which tempt and slay;
Religion Christless, Godless – a book sealed;
A senate, – Time's worst statue unrepealed, –
Are graves, from which a glorious Phantom may
Burst, to illumine our tempestuous day.

PERCY BYSSHE SHELLEY, 'England in 1819' (1819)

This is not disgust. Or at least, it is not only disgust. It is rage. In the form of a sonnet. Shelley creates the perfect form (a sonnet, but rhyming unconventionally abababcdcdccdd) to rail against the state of the nation.

It is not necessary to know who the dying king is (it was George III), or anything about the princes or rulers, in order to be able to appreciate Shelley's rage, because anyway he effectively kills off all of the poem's personages in his closing couplet, laying them, or rather tossing them – throwing them, making them literally – into graves ('Are graves').

We would draw attention also to the word 'burst', which tells you that In this present moment (1819) things can barely be constrained, as if everything – people, bodies, nation, the unconventional sonnet itself – is about to explode.

Shelley, unlike Wordsworth, has no need to appeal to any other person for authority: he is certainly not summoning the spirit of John Milton. Look around you, he says, look at the state of things: 'a glorious Phantom may / Burst to illumine our tempestuous day'. His invocation is to the nation itself.

(And we would point out also, in parenthesis, the field – this is a field guide after all. Note: 'A people starved and stabbed in the untilled field'. Such fields are part of poetry's remit: the field of conflict, the field of war.)

There may be an explosion:

58

it woz in April nineteen eighty-wan
doun inna di ghetto af Brixtan
dat di babylan dem cause such a frickshan
an it bring about a great insohreckshan
an it spread all ovah di naeshan
it woz a truly an histarical okayjan

it woz event af di year
an I wish I ad been dere
wen wi run riot all ovah Brixtan
wen wi mash-up plenty police van
wen wi mash-up di wicked wan plan
wen we mash-up di Swamp Eighty-wan
fi wha?
fi mek di rulah dem andahstan
dat wi naw tek noh more a dem oppreshan

LINTON KWESI JOHNSON, 'Di Great Insohreckshan' (1984)

It is not necessary to know who 'di wicked wan' was (it was
Margaret Thatcher), in order to be able to appreciate Linton
Kwesi Johnson's rage. It is audible in the rhyming: in 'frickshan',
'insohreckshan' and 'andahstan'. It is audible in the voice of the
poem, which insists on being what it is.

Kwesi Johnson's ambition? Surely, like MacDiarmid's, to write
'An exuberant, fustigating, truculent, polysyllabic' song. A song
truculent and polysyllabic enough to articulate 'insohreckshan'.

59

I think many people (like myself) prefer to read poetry mixed with prose; it gives you more to go by; the conventions of poetry have been getting far off from normal life, so that to have a prose bridge makes reading poetry seem more natural.

WILLIAM EMPSON, *The Complete Poems of William Empson*, ed. John Haffenden (2000)

Like Empson, and perhaps like many people, we too prefer to read poetry mixed with prose. And we're agreed, we think, in so far as we get the meaning, that poetry mixed with prose gives you 'more to go by'. Maybe what Empson means is that 'poetic' expression has its limits, and that to reach beyond them it has to lean on prose. If that's what he means, then we agree with him. We recommend, in this respect, most poets in this book.

As for whether 'the conventions of poetry are always getting far off from normal life', that's true, they are, and they always have. This will be on account of most people not transacting their business in poetic forms.

As to whether this is a good thing or a bad thing, that will depend on what 'normal life' is like. As for whether the 'normal', as Empson implies, is the natural: of that we are decidedly unsure.

Still, though, we're with Empson on most things, and certainly on the question of mixing: poetry shot through with prose is always better. Think of it as light relief. Or shading. Think of it, perhaps, as chiaroscuro.

As for whether prose is a bridge: prose *may* be a bridge.

But prose may also be the river, and poetry the bridge.

Or poetry the bridge, and poetry the river.

60

Consciousness is in constant change. I do not mean by this to say that no one state of mind has any duration—even if true, that would be hard to establish. What I wish to lay stress on is this, *that no state once gone can recur and be identical with what it was before.* Now we are seeing, now hearing; now reasoning, now willing; now recollecting, now expecting; now loving, now hating; and in a hundred other ways we know our minds to be alternately engaged. [...] The grass out of the window now looks to me of the same green in the sun as in the shade, and yet a painter would have to paint one part of it dark brown, another part bright yellow, to give it real sensational effect. We take no heed, as a rule, of the different way in which the same things look and sound and smell at different distances and under different circumstances. The sameness of the *things* is what we are concerned to ascertain; and any sensations that assure us of that will probably be considered in a rough way to be the same with each other. [...] From one year to another we see things in new lights. What was unreal has grown real, and what was exciting is insipid. The friends we used to care the world for are shrunken to shadows; the women once so divine, the stars, the woods, and the waters, how now so dull and common!—the young girls that brought an aura of infinity, at present hardly distinguishable existences; the pictures so empty; and as for the books, what was there to find so mysteriously significant in Goethe, or in John Mill so full of weight? Instead of all this, more zestful than ever is the work, the work; and fuller and deeper the import of common duties and of common goods.

WILLIAM JAMES, 'The Stream of Consciousness' (1892)

Look out of the window, James suggests, and see how various that field is. And look, now, see, how it differs from only an hour ago. There, he insists, in that variation, is what we should be interested in. Not, 'the sameness of things', not the 'rough way' in which things will 'be the same as each other'.

This is a tall order, and one we are not equal to, but one which

should be permitted to stimulate invention. James's invention –
or is it discovery (even as we type we cannot be sure, prone to
qualification as we are, and susceptible to new information) –
was the 'stream of consciousness'. If only we could keep pace
with the stream of consciousness, then we might appreciate
variation in all its forms.

Which means we must be quick. No, quicker. All things change.

Which raises the question, what, if anything, remains?

61 I've known rivers:
I've known rivers ancient as the world and older than the
flow of human blood in human veins.

My soul has grown deep like the rivers.

I bathed in the Euphrates when dawns were young.
I built my hut near the Congo and it lulled me to sleep.
I looked upon the Nile and raised the Pyramids above it.
I heard the singing of the Mississippi when Abe Lincoln
went down to New Orleans, and I've seen its muddy
bosom turn all golden in the sunset.

I've known rivers:
Ancient, dusky rivers.

My soul has grown deep like the rivers.

LANGSTON HUGHES, 'The Negro Speaks of Rivers' (1921)

Deep?

'Deep like the rivers'?

**Here is the teenage Langston Hughes – he was 17 when he wrote
this poem – claiming to be ancient. To do so he borrows his
cadences – and the rivers – from the Negro spiritual. What we
hear in 'The Negro Speaks of Rivers' is the sound of Negroes
speaking of rivers. The poem has echoes. It speaks with the force
of more than one voice. It reaches back in order to reach out.**

**Like Whitman, whom it echoes also, the poem claims identity with
those it speaks to. It founds that identity in blood, and in rivers.
Unlike in James, though, the point of these rivers is not that they
flow. Or at least, that if they do, they flow *back* to a common
source. The point of Hughes's river poem is not to establish change
but solidarity.**

But deep?

Deep?

62 I have grown weary of the poets, the old and the new: they all seem to me superficial and shallow seas.

They have not thought deeply enough: therefore their feeling – has not plumbed the depths.

A little voluptuousness and a little tedium: that is all their best ideas have ever amounted to.

All their harp-jangling is to me so much coughing and puffing of phantoms; what have they ever known of the ardour of tones!

They are not clean enough for me, either: they all disturb their waters so that they may seem deep!

FRIEDRICH NIETZSCHE, 'Of poets', *Thus Spoke Zarathustra* (1892), tr. R.J. Hollingdale

The question is – the question Nietzsche doesn't answer – is what, in writing, can possibly constitute 'deep'? Look at the writing in front of you. Where's the depth? Where can the depth possibly be? Is 'depth' not the oldest and deepest of all illusions? If we look for depth, are we not in danger of falling in? What is it, we ponder, deeply, when we look for depth in a poem, that we are hoping to find?

63

Some may ward off insomnia by reciting poetry to themselves, such as Tennyson's 'The moan of doves in immemorial elms, and murmuring of innumerable bees'. But this has never worked for me, because I invariably begin to take the lines of a poem apart. A friend of mine, fighting off the bells of Poe and avoiding the thickets of Eliot, manages to doze off after several repetitions of, to set it down in a long ramble, 'In Xanadu did Kubla Khan a stately pleasure dome decree, where Alph the sacred river ran through caverns measureless to man down to a sunless sea.' I tried that several times, discovered the solitary long O in 'dome', the six consecutive words containing R, and the last seven R-less words. The dome seemed to stick up a mile above the sunless sea, the rolling Rs trickled away, and I was left stranded in a desiccation of '... to man down to a sunless sea'.

JAMES THURBER, 'The Tyranny of Trivia', *Lanterns and Lances* (1961)

Indulge us, and allow us James Thurber to answer the question for us, and to speak truth back to Nietzsche: the depth of a poem is in its surface.

64

Thus:

Standing on the smooth sandy beach at the east end of the pond, in a calm September afternoon, when a slight haze makes the opposite shore line indistinct, I have seen whence came the expression, "the glassy surface of a lake." When you invert your head, it looks like a thread of finest gossamer stretched across the valley, and gleaming against the distant pine woods, separating one stratum of the atmosphere from another. You would think that you could walk dry under it to the opposite hills, and that the swallows which skim over might perch on it. Indeed, they sometimes dive below the line, as it were by mistake, and are undeceived. As you look over the pond westward you are obliged to employ both your hands to defend your eyes against the reflected as well as the true sun, for they are equally bright; and if, between the two, you survey its surface critically, it is literally as smooth as glass, except where the skater insects at equal intervals scattered over its whole extent, by their motions in the sun produce the finest imaginable sparkle on it, or, perchance, a duck plumes itself, or, as I have said, a swallow skims so low as to touch it. It may be that in the distance a fish describes an arc of three or four feet in the air, and there is one bright flash where it emerges, and another where it strikes the water; sometimes the whole silvery arc is revealed; or here and there, perhaps, is a thistle-down floating on its surface, which the fishes dart at and so dimple it again. It is like molten glass cooled but not congealed, and the few motes in it are pure and beautiful like imperfections in glass. You may often detect a yet smoother and darker water, separated from the rest as if by an invisible cobweb, boom of the water nymphs, resting on it. From a hill-top you can see a fish leap in almost any part; for not a pickerel or shiner picks an insect from this smooth surface but it manifestly disturbs the equilibrium of the whole lake. It is wonderful with what elaborateness this simple fact is advertised.

HENRY DAVID THOREAU, 'The Ponds', *Walden* (1854)

And so Thoreau speaks also to Nietzsche. As he spea
others (and to Empson, perhaps, in particular, for here, a
justification for mixing poetry with prose).

And look again: no depth, only more and more surface, the
continuing elaboration of what, when observing, it is possible
to see.

When Thoreau went to live in a hut by Walden Pond, in Concord,
Massachusetts, for two years between 1847 and 1849, it was partly
as an experiment in living. How little, he wondered, was it possible
to make do with? Not how *much*, note, but how little. Was it
possible, he asked himself, to have an existence which didn't
involve work?

But Thoreau's was also an experiment in language. Given time
and attention, he wanted to know, how much more equal might
writing be to its environment? How much more of nature, given
world enough and time, might writing be able to show?

And so, anyway, here is Thoreau, beside the pond, invoking not
depths but presenting surfaces, showing how, all the time, the
surface of the water is in a state of change. But see how he
registers that change also. Survey the surface of Thoreau's prose
critically. See how beautifully modulated are his sentences. Hear the
placement and variation of his sounds. Hear, for instance, the play
and variation of syllables in:

> except where the skater insects at equal intervals scattered
> over its whole extent, by their motions in the sun produce the
> finest imaginable sparkle on it.

This, to clarify – as if it were down to us, to clarify Thoreau –
is how one apprehends depths, or, rather, how poetry presents
fullness.

o5

I can lay down that history
I can lay down my glasses
I can lay down the imaginary lists
of what to forget and what must be
done. I can shake the sun
out of my eyes and lay everything down
on the hot sand, and cross
the whispering threshold and walk
right into the clear sea, and float there,
my long hair floating, and fishes
vanishing all around me. Deep water.
Little by little one comes to know
the limits and depths of power.

DENISE LEVERTOV, 'Action' (1958)

Denise Levertov was a typical American poet. She was from Ilford, in Essex, in England.

Little by little she comes to know things.

She floats in deep water.

66   My long two-pointed ladder's sticking through a tree
Toward heaven still.
And there's a barrel that I didn't fill
Beside it, and there may be two or three
Apples I didn't pick upon some bough.
But I am done with apple-picking now.
Essence of winter sleep is on the night,
The scent of apples; I am drowsing off.
I cannot shake the shimmer from my sight
I got from looking through a pane of glass
I skimmed this morning from the water-trough,
And held against the world of hoary grass.
It melted, and I let it fall and break.
But I was well
Upon my way to sleep before it fell,
And I could tell
What form my dreaming was about to take.
Magnified apples appear and disappear,
Stem end and blossom end,
And every fleck of russet showing clear.
My instep arch not only keeps the ache,
It keeps the pressure of a ladder-round.
I feel the ladder sway as the boughs bend
And I keep hearing from the cellar-bin
That rumbling sound
Of load on load of apples coming in.
For I have had too much
Of apple-picking; I am overtired
Of the great harvest I myself desired.
There were ten thousand thousand fruit to touch,
Cherish in hand, lift down, and not let fall,
For all
That struck the earth,
No matter if not bruised, or spiked with stubble,
Went surely to the cider-apple heap
As of no worth.
One can see what will trouble
This sleep of mine, whatever sleep it is.
Were he not gone,
The woodchuck could say whether it's like his

Long sleep, as I describe its coming on,
Or just some human sleep.

ROBERT FROST, 'After Apple-Picking' (1914)

Water here too, in this most well-known of Frost poems. But this time in the form of ice.

And apples of course, thousands and thousands of apples.

Then that strange line at the end: 'Or just some human sleep'.

This poem *is* what it seems. It is by and about a man who has picked too many apples. So many apples he is dreaming of them. So many trips up the ladder he can feel it in his feet. The poem is an articulation of what it is like to make a gesture too many times. 'I have had too much / Of apple-picking,' the farmer-poet says straightforwardly, 'I am overtired'.

But the poem is also not quite what it seems, or not simply anyway. Why, we should wonder, emphasize a 'human sleep' like that? The answer: that this is a poem about perspective. The poet tells us as much when he says, he 'cannot shake the shimmer from my sight'. It is a poem about being caught within a point of view.

And the point of view in question is the point of view of the Poet; not Frost, in particular, but the Poet in general. The point of view, that is to say, of the poet's language. Apples, in poetry, after all, are rarely just apples. They are almost always, rather, *apples*, bearing all the symbolic baggage heaped upon them since Adam and Eve ate from the tree of knowledge. An apple, by the time Frost writes (at the beginning of the 20th century), is no longer just an apple, just like a rose is no longer just a rose. Both are heavy with connotation, and the poet trying to make something of them finds himself heavy with sleep.

Or, as the poet George Oppen put it in 'Five Poems About Poetry':

> The question is: how does one hold an apple
> Who likes apples

Where the question is, how does one, as a poet, talk about apples without the *meaning* of apples getting in the way.

Frost was a congenial, apple-picking, farmer-poet, and a humanist sceptic. He is 'done with apple-picking', because poetic apple-picking has been too much done.

67

What wondrous life in this I lead!
Ripe Apples drop about my head;
The Luscious Clusters of the Vine
Upon my Mouth do crush their Wine;
The Nectaren, and curious Peach,
Into my hands themselves do reach;
Stumbling on Melons, as I pass,
Insnar'd with flowers, I fall on Grass.

ANDREW MARVELL, from 'The Garden' (1681)

Marvell is not tired of apple-picking, because he is not having to pick apples: ripe apples drop about his head.

Wondrous!

And then he trips and falls. On melons. He becomes 'Insnar'd with flowers'.

We shan't over-elaborate, but we take this as a warning about plenitude.

A warning, if we might say so, against poetic over-production. And critical over-explanation.

68

En robe de parade.
                    Samain

Like a skein of loose silk blown against a wall
She walks by the railing of a path in Kensington Gardens,
And she is dying piece-meal
             of a sort of emotional anaemia.

And round about there is rabble
Of the filthy, sturdy, unkillable infants of the very poor.
They shall inherit the earth.

In her is the end of breeding.
Her boredom is exquisite and excessive.
She would like someone to speak to her,
And is almost afraid that I
             will commit that indiscretion.

EZRA POUND, 'The Garden' (1916)

Ezra Pound in the garden now, but this time it is Kensington Gardens.

No apples. No grapes. No melons. No flowers.

The question is: who – poet or woman – thinks the 'infants of the very poor' are 'unkillable'?

The question is: what is 'the end of breeding'?

Or to put it another way, between 'breed' as a noun ('a distinctive stock of animals or plants'), and 'breed' as a verb ('mate and then produce offspring'), lies the whole history of class differentiation that the poet finds here, in this mini-tableau.

The trouble is, between distinction and vigour, he hardly knows where to put himself.

It is, perhaps, an occupational hazard.

69 They flee from me that sometime did me seek,
　　　　With naked foot stalking in my chamber.
I have seen them gentle, tame, and meek,
　　　　That now are wild, and do not remember
　　　　That sometime they put themselves in danger
　　　　　　To take bread at my hand, and now they range,
　　　　　　Busily seeking with a continual change.

Thanked be Fortune it hath been otherwise,
　　　　Twenty times better; but once in special,
In thin array, after a pleasant guise,
　　　　When her loose gown from her shoulders did fall,
　　　　And she me caught in her arms long and small,
　　　　　　And therewith all sweetly did me kiss,
　　　　　　And softly said, "Dear heart, how like you this?"

It was no dream: I lay broad waking.
　　　　But all is turned thorough my gentleness
Into a strange fashion of forsaking;
　　　　And I have leave to go of her goodness,
　　　　And she also to use newfangleness.
　　　　　　But since that I so kindly am served,
　　　　　　I fain would know what she hath deserved.

SIR THOMAS WYATT, 'They Flee From Me That Sometime Did Me
Seek' (1557)

**Here, in this fraught and very sexy poem, the poet does know
where to put himself; or did, for a while, until forsaken.**

**Now he is uncertain. 'I fain would know what she hath deserved.'
The speaker is genuinely perplexed.**

He was desired, and so desired, but now he has been abandoned.

He is bitter.

70

Because I liked you better
    Than suits a man to say,
It irked you, and I promised
    I'd throw the thought away.

To put the world between us
    We parted, stiff and dry:
'Farewell,' said you, 'forget me.'
    'Farewell, I will,' said I.

If e'er, where clover whitens
    The dead man's knoll, you pass,
And no tall flower to meet you
    Starts in the trefoiled grass,

Halt by the headstone shading
    The heart you have not stirred,
And say the lad that loved you
    Was one that kept his word.

A.E. HOUSMAN, 'Because I liked you better' (1936)

This is another fraught and sexy poem. But it is, somehow, a depressing poem.

Like a lot of poems, it effects the opposite of what it says. It forgets to remember to forget: 'the lad that loved you' does not forget his lover.

The poem is certainly not stiff and dry. It is deeply restless and unsettled – particularly, we find, around the clover whitening the dead man's knoll – and sticky with meaning. But it is spent: 'Because I *liked* you better'.

Housman is speaking of a love that dares not speak its name that spoke its name.

And in speaking met with rejection: 'Because I liked you better / Than suits a man to say'.

71

Where shall we find bonds of connection sufficiently strict to typify the affinity betwixt metrical and prose composition? They both speak by and to the same organs; the bodies in which both of them are clothed may be said to be of the same substance, their affections are kindred, and almost identical, not necessarily differing even in degree; poetry sheds no tears 'such as Angels weep', but natural and human tears; she can boast of no celestial ichor that distinguishes her vital juices from those of prose; the same human blood circulates through the veins of them both.

WILLIAM WORDSWORTH, Preface, *Lyrical Ballads* (1800)

Empson again (No. 59). But also Housman again. And also somehow Pound (No. 68).

Critics, poets, teachers, lecturers, and other people who like to think themselves intimate with the minds and lives of the gods, like to pretend that poetry does indeed possess some kind of 'celestial ichor' distinguishable, under analysis, from the lovely 'vital juices' of prose. But there is no ichor; no blue blood; no Holy Grail; no blood line. Wordsworth, who claimed to speak to and for an ordinary audience, insists on mingling. 'The same human blood,' to pursue the metaphor, 'circulates through the veins of them both.'

72

I am a Jew. Hath not a Jew eyes? Hath not a Jew hands, organs, dimensions, senses, affections, passions? fed with the same food, hurt with the same weapons, subject to the same diseases, healed by the same means, warmed and cooled by the same winter and summer, as a Christian is? If you prick us do we not bleed? if you tickle us do we not laugh? if you poison us do we not die? and if you wrong us, shall we not revenge? If we are like you in the rest, we will resemble you in that. If a Jew wrong a Christian, what is his humility? Revenge. If a Christian wrong a Jew, what should his sufferance be by Christian example? Why, revenge. The villainy you teach me I will execute, and it shall go hard but I will better the instruction.

WILLIAM SHAKESPEARE, *The Merchant of Venice*, III.i.49–61 (1595)

Shylock refutes it. He also confirms it. No celestial ichor.

73

Why do you play such dreary music
on Saturday afternoon, when tired
mortally tired I long for a little
reminder of immortal energy?
                                        All
week long while I trudge fatiguingly
from desk to desk in the museum
you spill your miracles of Grieg
and Honegger on shut-ins.
                                        Am I not
shut in too, and after a week
of work don't I deserve Prokofieff?

Well, I have my beautiful de Kooning
to aspire to. I think it has an orange
bed in it, more than the ear can hold.

FRANK O'HARA, 'Radio' (1955)

O'Hara refutes it also. No celestial ichor here either.

Longing, on Saturday afternoon, for 'a little / reminder of immortal energy', it is to his radio that O'Hara turns, calling on it to spill miracles of Grieg and Honegger, just as it does through the working week.

No ichor, then, and no invocation; just an appeal to popular broadcasting. Poetry, as Wordsworth insists It should be, to be vitalized by another medium.

And the word Is 'spill', which for Barrett Browning (No. 39) and for Yeats (No. 40) meant wastage, but which for O'Hara rhymes with 'miracle', and which for him means the most fluid, unboundaried exchange.

Everything spills. The radio spills its miracles. O'Hara spills those same miracles to the reader. The poem, informed by prose, allows sense to spill over the end of the lines.

But then this was 1950s America, and everything was spilt.

Charlie Parker spilt solos. Jackson Pollock spilt paint. O'Hara, himself, when he wasn't writing his rapidly beautiful poems, gave most of his time to circulating the work of those – like Pollock – among his contemporaries he most admired.

The phrase for this is from Longinus: O'Hara, above all things, shared his enthusiasms.

74

What the ear can hold:

What art is, you know as well as I do: it is nothing more than rhythm. And if that's true, I don't have to burden myself with imitation or with soul, but can modestly and simply give you rhythm, in any material whatsoever: bus tickets, oil paints, building blocks, that's right, you heard me, building blocks, or words in poetry, or sounds in music, or you just name it. That's why you mustn't look too hard at the material; because that isn't what it's all about. Don't look for some hidden imitation of nature, don't ask about expressions of the soul, but try, in spite of the unusual materials, to catch the rhythm of the forms and the colors. This has about as much to do with bolshevism as a flapper's hairdo. It is, however, the essence of all art, i.e., that every artwork throughout history has had to fulfil this primary requirement: to be rhythm, or else it isn't art.

KURT SCHWITTERS, '(What art is, you know …)', *Poems Performance Pieces Proses Plays Poetics*, ed. Jerome Rothenberg (1994)

But the question is: what is rhythm?

75 David kept writing songs. A lot of them. In the beginning of 1974, he wrote what would prove to be his signature song, "Psycho Killer" [...]. David Byrne's voicing of America's passion of homicide was inspired by a twenty-four-year-old girl named Barbar Conway. [...] She called cool people and situations "psycho killer." [...] Around Thanksgiving '73, David heard Barbara say "psycho killer" for the zillionth time and finally thought, "There's a song here." [...] As David begins singing, his killer addresses the listener directly, revealing that he is in denial ("I can't seem to face up to the facts"), that he's wired, an insomniac. In case we miss the point, the killer announces, "Don't touch me I'm a real live wire." Then the psycho killer begins speaking French, *"Psycho killer, qu'est-ce que c'est?"*

Paul McCartney speaks French in "Michelle" to give the song a fake sophistication. One version of history says David's psycho speaks in French because the maniac imagines himself as very refined. Another because of his split personality. A third story says David originally wanted the guy to speak Greek, but was convinced that French was a more suitable language for someone who was disturbed.

Chris told David, "Hey, Tina speaks French. She'll help with the lyrics." [...]

Tina contributed more than French to the song. Both she and Chris were Otis Redding freaks. Redding was a Stax recording artist best known for his '68 hit, "(Sittin' on) The Dock of the Bay." Two years before he released a single called "Fa-Fa-Fa-Fa-Fa (Sad Song)." It's a relaxed song. Otis tells us that he keeps singing sad songs. They're all he knows. But this particular sad song is a sweet song as well. Anyone can sing it. *Fa-Fa-Fa-Fa-Fa.*

The story goes that after Chris and Tina played it for David, he incorporated a string of *fa*s in his psycho killer song. He sang that short syllable *fa* – a simple exhalation of breath, with upper teeth pressed against lower lip, ten times:

fa fa fa fa fa fa fa fa fa fa

Otis Redding may or may not have been an influence, but there is a problem of pronunciation. The real influence on the fas in "Psycho Killer" probably came from The Kinks' song "David Watts," which begins with Ray Davies singing:

fa fa fa fa fa fa fa fa

David would pronounce his *fa* the same as Davies.

This slight one-symbol word has a maddening mystery connected to it. When the song was released in 1977, the printed lyrics appeared with only six *fa*s. But on the actual record, as well as in concert, Byrne sang ten *fa*s. Bootlegs reveal that David Byrne experimented constantly with the rhythm of his *fa*s in the early days. A few times he sang seven fas. Other times he did a kind of speeded-up string of them, sputtering his *fa*s like Porky Pig's famous line, "Tha-tha-tha-that's all folks." But he never sang six *fa*s. The mystery may never be explained.

DAVID BOWMAN, *fa fa fa fa fa fa: The Adventures of Talking Heads in the 20th Century* (2001)

That's rhythm. And so is this:

76   When that I was and a little tiny boy,
        With hey, ho, the wind and the rain;
A foolish thing was but a toy,
        For the rain it raineth every day.

But when I came to man's estate,
        With hey, ho, the wind and the rain;
'Gainst knaves and thieves men shut their gates,
        For the rain it raineth every day.

But when I came, alas! to wive,
        With hey, ho, the wind and the rain;
By swaggering could I never thrive,
        For the rain it raineth every day.

But when I came unto my beds,
        With hey, ho, the wind and the rain;
With toss-pots still had drunken heads,
        For the rain it raineth every day.

A great while ago the world begun,
        With hey, ho, the wind and the rain;
But that's all one, our play is done,
        And we'll strive to please you every day.

WILLIAM SHAKESPEARE, *Twelfth Night*, V.i.401–20 (1600?)

Fa fa fa fa fa fa fa fa fa fa.

Hey, ho?

The *OED* offers this: 'An utterance, app. of nautical origin, and marking the rhythm of movement in heaving or hauling'.

This is what poems do: mark the rhythm of movement in heaving or hauling.

'Hey, ho' also offers an attitude, a two-syllable guide to sustainable living; a way – 'hey, ho' – of carrying on. Not happily, necessarily, but not dismissively either. Shakespeare's 'hey, ho' is not a 'whatever'. It's more like, say, 'tra-la':

77 In the first taxi he was alone tra-la,
No extras on the clock. He tipped ninepence
But the cabby, while he thanked him, looked askance
As though to suggest someone had bummed a ride.

In the second taxi he was alone tra-la
But the clock showed sixpence extra; he tipped according
And the cabby from out of his muffler said: 'Make sure
You have left nothing behind tra-la between you.'

In the third taxi he was alone tra-la
But the tip-up seats were down and there was an extra
Charge of one-and-sixpence and an odd
Scent that reminded him of a trip to Cannes.

As for the fourth taxi, he was alone
Tra-la when he hailed it but the cabby looked
Through him and said: 'I can't tra-la well take
So many people, not to speak of the dog.'

LOUIS MACNEICE, 'The Taxis' (1961)

The apparently throwaway tra-la here is in fact the whole point
of the poem. It's the punchline. MacNeice is writing a kind of
music-hall skit.

The poem goes tra-la, tra-la, tra-la, and then 'I can't tra-la well
take / So many people, not to speak of the dog', meaning, in other
words, no longer merely tra-la, but rather 'I can't *flipping* well (or
bloody well, or *blinking* well, or *blasted* well, or whatever two-
syllable curse or expletive you prefer) take / So many people, not
to speak of the dog'.

The dog, the post-punchline, is also very funny. He is also,
presumably, Cerberus.

78 One more rhythm:

Whan that Aprill with his shoures soote
The droghte of March hath perced to the roote,
And bathed every veyne in swich licour
Of which vertu engendred is the flour;
Whan Zephirus eke with his swete breeth
Inspired hath in every holt and heeth
The tendre croppes, and the yonge sonne
Hath in the Ram his halfe cours yronne,
And smale foweles maken melodye,
That slepen al the nyght with open ye
(So pricketh hem nature in hir corages),
Thanne longen folk to goon on pilgrimages,
And palmeres for to seken straunge strondes,
To ferne halwes, kowthe in sondry londes;
And specially from every shires ende
Of Engelond, to Caunterbury they wende,
The hooly blisful martir for to seke,
That hem hath holpen whan that they were seeke.

GEOFFREY CHAUCER, General Prologue, *The Canterbury Tales*, ll.1–18
(*c*.1387)

Don't be shy.

Read this aloud.

Say 'droghte'. Say 'perced'. Say 'croppes'. Say 'yronne'.

See how it makes the language newly strange?

See how it makes other poems in the language more vivid?

Say it.

'April is the cruellest month.'

79 Work begins long before one receives or is aware of a social command.

Preliminary work goes on incessantly.

You can produce good poetic work to order only when you've a very large stock of preliminaries behind you. [...]

All my time goes on these preliminaries. I spend from ten to eighteen hours each day on them, and I'm almost always muttering something or other. My concentration on them accounts for my notorious poetic absent-mindedness.

VLADIMIR MAYAKOVSKY, *How Are Verses Made?* (1926), tr. G.M. Hyde

Let's imagine for a moment that you are a Mayakovskyan poet. You may well be a Mayakovskyan poet: a poet of grand Mayakovskyan dreams and determinations.

So do you spend between ten and eighteen hours a day on preparing yourself to write poetry?

No?

In which case, you are not really a Mayakovskyan poet at all, are you?

80

Somewhere, even now, on the banks of the Severn, the Thames, the Trent, the Great Ouse, the Wye, the Tay, the Spey, the Clyde, the Tweed, the Nene, the Eden, the Avon, the Teme, the Lagan, the Liffey, the Don, the Bann, the Ribble, the Tyne, the Tees, the Mersey, the Dee, the Danube, the Yangtze, the Nile, the Congo, the Ganges, the Hudson, the Jordan, the Mississippi, the poem on the preceding page is being written.

Epic in scope, devastating in implication, unashamed by its own adventure, naked in its ambition, full with possibilities, raging, generous, beautiful and provocative, the poem speaks to all men and women in a voice tuned to a less impoverished future.

Are you writing this poem?

If so, please contact *The Enthusiast*, and we will be pleased to include it here in future editions.

There are no restrictions on line length, subject matter or form.

81

Light:

There's a certain Slant of light,
Winter Afternoons—
That oppresses, like the Heft
Of Cathedral Tunes—

Heavenly Hurt, it gives us—
We can find no scar,
But internal difference,
Where the Meanings, are—

None may teach it—Any—
'Tis the Seal Despair—
An imperial affliction
Sent us of the Air—

When it comes, the Landscape listens—
Shadows—hold their breath—
When it goes, 'tis like the Distance
On the look of Death—

EMILY DICKINSON, Poem 258 (c.1861)

Emily Dickinson throws light on meaning.

In April 1862 Dickinson wrote to the essayist and critic Thomas Wentworth Higginson. Higginson had just published an article in the *Atlantic Monthly* entitled 'Letter to a Young Contributor'. In her letter to Higginson, Dickinson had one question: 'Are you too deeply occupied to say if my Verse is alive?'

Higginson was not too deeply occupied, but he was too deeply conservative, and though he was aware of something valuable in Dickinson's faltering, enigmatic, passive-aggressive hymn-like poems, he advised her against publication.

Duly discouraged, Dickinson only published a handful of poems in her lifetime. After her death her poems began to see the light of day, but in mangled form – early editors correcting what they took to be her mistaken punctuation.

But Dickinson punctuated the way she wanted to. She met with rejection because she insisted on her own terms. The dashes –

they're deliberate. They make the poem halting and hesitant. They articulate the difficulty Dickinson had in saying what she meant.

And she had difficulty saying what she meant because, as she saw it, meaning is difficult. Here, in Poem 258 – her poems didn't have titles – she tries to catch the significance of a certain slant of light. We think we know what she means, and she helps us with her cathedral simile. The light is heavy, dark with meaning.

But the meaning of the poem isn't straightforwardly public, it is partly private to herself. She wants to get it across to us, but she can't, and so what she conveys instead is the difficulty of communication; the semi-privacy of 'internal difference / Where the meanings, are—'.

A Dickinson poem is an exercise in honest speaking.

82 Into dark:

Not every man has gentians in his house
in soft September, at slow, sad Michaelmas.

Bavarian gentians, big and dark, only dark
darkening the day-time torch-like with the smoking
    blueness of Pluto's gloom,
ribbed and torch-like, with their blaze of darkness spread
    blue
down flattening into points, flattened under the sweep of
    white day
torch-flower of the blue-smoking darkness, Pluto's dark-
    blue daze,
black lamps from the halls of Dis, burning dark blue,
giving off darkness, blue darkness, as Demeter's pale
    lamps give off light,
lead me then, lead me the way.

Reach me a gentian, give me a torch
let me guide myself with the blue, forked torch of this
    flower
down the darker and darker stairs, where blue is darkened
    on blueness,
even where Persephone goes, just now, from the frosted
    September
to the sightless realm where darkness is awake upon the
    dark
and Persephone herself is but a voice
or a darkness invisible enfolded in the deeper dark
of the arms Plutonic, and pierced with the passion of
    dense gloom,
among the splendour of torches of darkness, shedding
    darkness on the lost bride and her groom.

D.H. LAWRENCE, 'Bavarian Gentians' (1932)

**It may help to know that Emily Dickinson wrote a poem – which
we have not quoted – which begins 'God made a little Gentian'.
Dickinson's gentian was *gentiana crinita* or *gentiana ciliata*.**

It may help to know that D.H. Lawrence's gentian is the *gentiana bavarica*, a plant of temperate and mountainous regions with violet or blue trumpet-shaped flowers.

It may help to know that Lawrence wrote his gentian poem shortly before his death. He was ill with tuberculosis, and staying in the Alpine village of Rottach-am-Tegernsee. The poem was published posthumously.

And it may help to know that, at the end there, the lost bride and her groom are Eurldyce and Orpheus, the poet of myth descended to the underworld to seek out his love.

But it may be most helpful of all to note that in this poem it is 'dark' no fewer than six times, 'darkening' once, 'darker' twice, 'darkened' once, and 'darkness' eight times. Lawrence is descending into darkness.

Not every man, the poem remarks (truly), has gentians in his house. In this, at least, the poet is fortunate. But fortunate how? Because the gentians in their darkness – as soft measures of darkness – may serve, perhaps, in their darkness, to ease the poet to his death.

'Reach me a gentian,' he says, because he cannot reach one for himself. And slowly, *slowly,* the lights go out. And gradually the flower, depicted longingly at first, slips into the background, leaving the poet in 'the deeper dark'.

'Not every man has gentians in his house / in soft September, at slow, sad Michaelmas.'

83 In the staring darkness
I can hear the harshness
Of the cold wind blowing.
I am warmly clad,
And I'm very glad
That I've got a home.

GERARD MANLEY HOPKINS, Fragment 132 (*c*.1862–68)

Not 'a house', 'a home'.

Discuss.

84

It is this deep blankness is the real thing strange.
The more things happen to you the more you can't
Tell or remember even what they were.

The contradictions cover such a range.
The talk would talk and go so far aslant.
You don't want madhouse and the whole thing there.

WILLIAM EMPSON, 'Let it Go' (1940)

Here is William Empson saying what T.S. Eliot said in 'Burnt Norton', *Four Quartets*, that 'human kind cannot bear very much reality'; or as Empson puts it, more elliptically, 'the real thing strange'.

The poem works by its slight distortions, by the minor glitches in its syntax: the repetition of 'is' in the first line; the appearance of 'madhouse', not madness, in the last. The feeling is of a person just holding on, which is, perhaps, why the advice is to 'Let it go' – because the alternative to letting it go is 'madhouse and the whole thing there'.

And maybe we should notice that word 'aslant', and maybe we should remember Emily Dickinson, who remarked on 'a certain Slant of light' (No. 81), and whose injunction in another poem (1129) was to 'Tell all the truth but tell it slant'. Any other way would be overwhelming, risking what Empson called 'this deep blankness'. Or as Dickinson put it:

The truth must dazzle gradually
Or every man be blind—

85 The night is darkening round me
The wild winds coldly blow
But a tyrant spell has bound me
And I cannot cannot go

The giant trees are bending
Their bare boughs weighed with snow
The storm is fast descending
And yet I cannot go

Clouds beyond clouds above me
Wastes beyond wastes below
But nothing drear can move me
I will not cannot go

EMILY BRONTË, 'The night is darkening round me' (1837)

Again with the darkness, and again with the wind blowing, but Emily Brontë is not warmly clad and there is no sign of home. She is fixed, but nothing else is. She is surrounded by chaos. And in the chaos she endeavours to keep hold of herself.

The poem turns on 'Me's and 'I's, as if by repeating pronouns she can maintain herself. But the poem lacks will, and the pronouns are barely sufficient. The world, in its strangeness, has run to excess.

86

Because:

Definition is indeed, not the province of man: everything is set above or below our faculties. The works and operations of nature are too great in their extent, or too much diffused in their relations, and the performances of art too inconsistent and uncertain, to be reduced to any determinate idea. [...] Definitions have been no less difficult or uncertain in criticisms than in law. Imagination [...] has always endeavoured to baffle the logician, to perplex the confines of distinction, and burst the inclosures of regularity.

SAMUEL JOHNSON, *Rambler*, No. 125 (28 May 1751)

The phrase is 'burst the inclosures of regularity'.

Even so:

87

One of two kinds of clearness one should have – either the meaning to be felt without effort as fast as one reads or else, if dark at first reading, when once made out *to explode.*

GERARD MANLEY HOPKINS, *Letters of Gerard Manley Hopkins*, ed. C.C. Abbott (1955)

See, for instance, as an example of exploding clarity, Hopkins's inclosure-bursting sonnet 'The Windhover', and especially the first three lines of the poem's sestet:

> Brute beauty and valour and act, oh, air, pride, plume, here
>   Buckle! AND the fire that breaks from thee then, a billion
> Times told lovelier, more dangerous, O my chevalier!

The explosion is there in the word 'Buckle!', the moment in the poem when, for Hopkins, the physical world cracks under the strain of its spiritual meaning, and what he experiences is not the kestrel hovering but the divinity ('a billion / Times told lovelier') which hovers behind it.

The exploding poem is a revelation, a sudden manifestation of clarity.

Quieter moments of clarity are perhaps preferable.

As here:

Comes then snow scur on the river
And a world is covered with jade
Small boat floats like a lanthorn,
The flowing water clots as with cold. And at San Yin
they are a people of leisure.
Wild geese swoop to the sand-bar,
Clouds gather about the hole of the window
Broad water; geese line out with the autumn
Rooks clatter over the fishermen's lanthorns,
A light moves on the north sky line;
where the young boys prod stones for shrimp.
In seventeen hundred came Tsing to these hill lakes.
A light moves on the south sky line.

EZRA POUND, Canto XLIX (1937)

Where the trick is the equal distribution of emphasis, so that on each and every thing the poem, as it were, sheds its light: on the 'snow scur', and on the 'geese', and on the 'rooks', and on the 'shrimp'. This is the value of free verse. In the absence of metre the poem's emphasis falls everywhere. Everything, so Pound would have us believe, is illuminated. The key element of poetry, he argued, is light.

89

Or here, where:

I found a ball of grass among the hay
And progged it as I passed and went away;
And when I looked I fancied something stirred,
And turned again and hoped to catch the bird—
When out an old mouse bolted in the wheats
With all her young ones hanging at her teats;
She looked so odd and so grotesque to me,
I ran and wondered what the thing could be,
And pushed the knapweed bunches where I stood;
Then the mouse hurried from the craking brood.
The young ones squeaked, and as I went away
She found her nest again among the hay.
The water o'er the pebbles scarce could run
And broad old cesspools glittered in the sun.

JOHN CLARE, 'Mouse's Nest' (*c.*1832–37)

This poem doesn't burst or explode; it wanders in, and then wanders off.

See how the poet fancies he sees a bird, and how then in reality the bird is a mouse. And how the mouse looks so 'grotesque and odd' that the poet has to go over and have a look; and how having looked he goes away. And then how, in the closing couplet, the mouse has disappeared altogether, and instead we are given 'cesspools' which 'glittered in the sun'.

It is a beautiful poem, a poem about looking, a poem attentive to its own attention: which wanders, and in wandering

stumbles across things.

90 the lilac moon of the earth's backyard
which gives silence to the whole house
falls down
out of the sky
over the fence

                        poor planet
                    now reduced
                    to disuse

who looks so big
and alive
I am talking to you

                    The shades
                    on the windows
                    of the Centers'
                    place
                    half down
                    like nobody else's
                    lets the glass lower halves
                    make quiet mouths at you

lilac moon

                    old backyard bloom

CHARLES OLSON, 'May 31, 1961'

And so here we are, on May 31, 1961, quietly watching. The moon
is big, and alive, and silent. Maybe it really was *lilac* as well. But it
is lilac partly because Charles Olson remembers Whitman. For
whom, as he contemplated the funeral of Abraham Lincoln, 'lilacs
last in the dooryard bloom'd'.

Since when, 'lilac' and 'lilacs' have been part of the American poet's
vocabulary. John Ashbery refers to 'the lake a lilac cube' in his
poem '"They Dream Only of America"'. Part of the pleasure of
Olson's poem is the way he makes the lilac fresh. Which is an effect,
if you like

            of the way he spaces.

Of the way, in the poem, the attention

                            falls.

91 In Leonardo's light
we questioned

the sun does not love
My hat

attained
the weight falls

I am at rest
You too

hold a doctorate
in Warmth

*

You are my friend—
you bring me peaches
and the high bush cranberry
                    you carry
my fishpole

you water my worms
you patch my boot
with your mending kit
            nothing in it
but my hand.

LORINE NIEDECKER, 'In Leonardo's light' and 'You are my friend'
from *Poems 1960–1964*

And falls again: this time on 'peaches' and 'the high cranberry bush'; 'fishpole', 'boot' and 'hand'.

92

And again, this time in Boston, where the cigarette, now, is
a torch:

> I sit in the evening, not on it
> this time the back porch of a building, designed in 1933,
> the year when conceived, enjoying clear twilight breeze.
> Finished a bottle of coke, and my last cigarette, before retiring,
> a blind man stumbles out, tapping his cane loudly.

JOHN WIENERS, 'Espionage' (1970)

Stumbles.

There is a whole poetics in that stumbling; stumbling *in*, stumbling *off*.

And stumbling *on*, which is to say not seeking but finding.

Poets who *stumble* write what they happen across.

93 Lead, kindly light, amid the encircling gloom,
　　　　Lead thou me on;
The night is dark, and I am far from home;
　　　　Lead thou me on.
Keep thou my feet; I do not ask to see
The distant scene: one step enough for me.

I was not ever thus, nor prayed that thou
　　　　Shouldst lead me on;
I loved to choose and see my path; but now
　　　　Lead thou me on.
I loved the garish day, and, spite of fears,
Pride ruled my will: remember not past years.

So long thy power hath blest me, sure it still
　　　　Will lead me on
O'er moor and fen, o'er crag and torrent, till
　　　　The night is gone,
And with the morn those angel faces smile
Which I have loved long since, and lost awhile.

JOHN HENRY NEWMAN, 'Lead, Kindly Light' (1833), from *The Revised Psalter*

Emily Dickinson, sceptical American Calvinist, wrote fractured hymns. John Henry Newman, English Catholic convert, wrote actual hymns.

The difference lies, we might point out, in the matter of choice.

Dickinson chose her terms of engagement; she asserted, at all times, the radical independence of her will. By contrast here's John Henry, latterly Cardinal, Newman, acknowledging that, once, 'I loved to choose and see my path', but now insisting that he does 'not ask to see'.

This hymn works by the refrain, by the insistence and reassuring repetition of the central appeal. It works also by not upsetting the apple-cart linguistically speaking; to do otherwise, to invent, would be to allow pride to rule the will. And so the will of the poet is submerged in familiar phrases: 'moor', 'torrent', 'crag' and 'fen'. There is no actual landscape here, just a set of iconographic obstacles over which 'the kindly light' will lead him.

Thump, thump goes the song, as it insists on its cadences.

It steps without seeing. But it doesn't *stumble.*

94

Another song:

Who would true Valour see,
Let him come hither;
One here will Constant be,
Come Wind, come Weather.
There's no Discouragement,
Shall make him once Relent,
His first avow'd Intent,
To be a Pilgrim.

Who so beset him round,
With dismal Storys,
Do but themselves confound;
His strength the more is.
No Lyon can him fright,
He'l with a Gyant Fight,
But he will have a right,
To be a Pilgrim.

Hobgoblin nor foul Fiend,
Can daunt his Spirit:
He knows, he at the end,
Shall Life Inherit.
Then Fancies fly away,
He'll fear not what men say,
He'll labour Night and Day,
To be a Pilgrim.

JOHN BUNYAN, 'The Pilgrim Song' (1678)

The crucial line here? 'His strength the *more* is.'

Why?

Because there – in the faith that increases in proportion to the obstacles thrown before it – is the whole history of evangelical persistence. Like the Pilgrim fathers who settled the northeastern seaboard of America, Bunyan saw in the test a sign: a sign that, like the persecuted Jews of the Old Testament, they had been chosen by God. Which makes one wonder, of course,

what a negative sign might look like. The 'garish day' perhaps – any evidence that here on earth things were going well.

Things didn't go worldly-well for Bunyan. He spent 12 years in jail for preaching without a licence, a sentence that was commuted from three months because he precisely refused to relent. He wrote the words of the hymn – which come from *The Pilgrim's Progress* – while in jail; and in his acceptance of his sentence announced himself as good as his word.

He could be as good as his word because his word had an underwriter.

His word, that is, was with God.

After God the good word calls for a different kind of earning.

As when, for instance:

95 The greatest plumber
in all the town
from Montgomery Ward
rode a Cadillac carriage
by marriage
and visited my pump

A sensitive pump
said he
that has at times a proper
balance
of water, air
and poetry.

LORINE NIEDECKER, 'Nursery Rhyme' (1970)

No god here, only 'balance', and, accordingly, a lighter song. And no symbols, except perhaps if you count the 'Cadillac carriage', which the plumber rides 'by marriage'. This poem, one might speculate, has the poise of things.

It also has a politics. Lorine Niedecker wrote about the things she found around her, where those things were things she came across as a labouring woman in Black Hawk Island, Wisconsin. Her 'Nursery Rhyme' about her 'pump' recalls William Carlos Williams's 'Red Wheelbarrow'; poems about things that 'so much depends upon'.

96 Should auld acquaintance be forgot
        And never brought to mind?
Should auld acquaintance be forgot,
        And auld lang syne!

For auld lang syne my jo,
        For auld lang syne,
We'll tak a cup o' kindness yet,
        For auld lang syne.

And surely ye'll be your pint-stowp!
        And surely I'll be mine!
And we'll tak a cup o' kindness yet
        For auld lang syne.

We twa hae run about the braes,
        And pou'd the gowans fine;
But we've wander'd mony a weary fitt,
        Sin' auld lang syne.

We twa hae paidl'd in the burn,
        From morning sun till dine;
But seas between us braid hae roar'd
        Sin' auld lang syne.

And there's a hand, my trusty fiere!
        And gie's a hand o' thine!
And we'll tak a right gude-willie waught,
        For auld lang syne.

ROBERT BURNS, 'For auld lang syne' (1793)

Here is Immanuel Kant not writing about Robert Burns: 'In all beautiful art the essential thing is the form.'

And here is T.S. Eliot, not writing about Robert Burns also: 'All art emulates the condition of ritual. That is what it comes from and to that it must always return for nourishment.'

97 Come live with me and be my Love,
And we will all the pleasures prove
That hills and valleys, dales and fields,
Or woods or steepy mountain yields.

And we will sit upon the rocks,
And see the shepherds feed their flocks
By shallow rivers, to whose falls
Melodious birds sing madrigals.

And I will make thee beds of roses
And a thousand fragrant posies;
A cap of flowers, and a kirtle
Embroidered all with leaves of myrtle.

A gown made of the finest wool
Which from our pretty lambs we pull;
Fair-lined slippers for the cold,
With buckles of the purest gold.

A belt of straw and ivy-buds,
With coral clasps and amber studs:
And if these pleasures may thee move,
Come live with me and be my Love.

The shepherd swains shall dance and sing
For thy delight each May morning:
If these delights thy mind may move,
Then live with me and be my Love.

CHRISTOPHER MARLOWE, 'The Passionate Shepherd to his Love' (*c.*1590)

This poem is included in many – if not most – anthologies of English poetry designed for school, university and personal use.

We would point to a particular:

kirtle n. archaic 1 a woman's gown or outer petticoat. 2 a man's tunic or coat. [Origin OE cyrtel, of Gmc origin, prob. based on L. *curtus* short.]

And add:

'The machinations of ambiguity are among the very roots of poetry' (William Empson, *Seven Types of Ambiguity*).

98

O western wynd, when wilt thou blow
And the small rain down shall rain
O Christ that my love were in my arms
And I in my bed again

ANONYMOUS, 'Western Wynd' (c.1500)

Concision, clearly, is this poem's virtue.

It may be short, but it contains everything: the weather, sex, religion, imagination and longing.

It is perhaps no coincidence that the poet is dreaming of lying in bed, for in a bed is our concision: in a bed we are born, sleep, dream, love and die.

'And I in my bed again'.

99

Winter is icummen in,
Lhude sing Goddamm,
Raineth drop and staineth slop,
And how the wind doth ramm!
                    Sing: Goddamm.
Skiddeth bus and sloppeth us,
An ague hath my ham.
Freezeth river, turneth liver,
                    Damn you, sing: Goddamm.
Goddamm, Goddamm, 'tis why I am, Goddamm,
                    So 'gainst the winter's balm.
Sing goddamm, damm, sing Goddamm,
Sing goddamm, sing goddamm, DAMM.

EZRA POUND, 'Ancient Music' (1916)

Ezra Pound liked concision: 'A Chinaman said long ago that if a man can't say what he has to say in twelve lines he had better keep quiet.'

Which produced a problem. 'I am often asked,' he said, in a note at the end of his essay on Vorticism, 'whether there can be a long imagiste or vorticist poem.' At the time of writing he didn't have an answer, or he didn't say what his answer was. *The Cantos*, however, in all its fragments, is a long imagiste poem.

Pound also liked a joke. 'Ancient Music' is his joke.

It is a thing easily forgotten, perhaps, that Modernism was capable of a sense of humour.

100

Lana Turner has collapsed!
I was trotting along and suddenly
it started raining and snowing
and you said it was hailing
but hailing hits you on the head
hard so it was really snowing and
raining and I was in such a hurry
to meet you but the traffic
was acting exactly like the sky
and suddenly I see a headline
LANA TURNER HAS COLLAPSED!
there is no snow in Hollywood
there is no rain in California
I have been to lots of parties
and acted perfectly disgraceful
but I never actually collapsed
oh Lana Turner we love you get up.

FRANK O'HARA, 'Poem' (1962)

So, now, Frank O'Hara wrote this poem on his way to a reading
with Robert Lowell on Staten Island on 9 February 1962. He then
read the poem that he had just written at the reading, and opinion
is divided as to whether he did so in order to pique the famously
studious and revisionary Lowell.

'I think there's been some misunderstanding,' writes Joe LeSueur,
'about Frank's attitude toward Lowell; he didn't like the guy's
poetry but he had nothing against him personally. Thus, and I'm
quite sure about this, at their joint reading he didn't try to show
Lowell up or tweak his nose in public by reading the Lana Turner
poem he'd written on the way to the reading. It's simply not the
sort of thing Frank would have done.'

What O'Hara did do, all the time, was write poems born in and of the
moment, determined to catch the impression of the there and the
then. Always he was in a hurry, because always there was a new
poem to write; because always – witness the weather, which even as
he describes he has to re-describe – things are in a state of flux.

As for Lana Turner, O'Hara is shocked. He has been to lots of parties, and acted perfectly disgraceful, but he has never *actually* collapsed. His poem, like so many of his poems, is an injunction to carry on: whatever the weather, because of the weather, no matter what.

101

Rain, midnight rain, nothing but the wild rain
On this bleak hut, and solitude, and me
Remembering again that I shall die
And neither hear the rain nor give it thanks
For washing me cleaner than I have been
Since I was born into this solitude.
Blessed are the dead that the rain rains upon:
But here I pray that none whom once I loved
Is dying tonight or lying still awake
Solitary, listening to the rain,
Either in pain or thus in sympathy
Helpless among the living and the dead,
Like a cold water among broken reeds,
Myriads of broken reeds all still and stiff,
Like me who have no love which this wild rain
Has not dissolved except the love of death,
If love it be towards what is perfect and
Cannot, the tempest tells me, disappoint.

EDWARD THOMAS, 'Rain' (1917)

'Rain' was written while Edward Thomas was preparing to go to
the front in 1917. He can find no consolation as he composes in
his bleak hut, except perhaps in death, because, of all things, death
will not disappoint. The question is, whether in its situational
melancholy Edward Thomas's poem invalidates Frank O'Hara's
poem written on the hoof.

The answer, of course, is 'No'.

102 I cannot tell you how it was;
But this I know: it came to pass
Upon a bright and breezy day
When May was young; ah, pleasant May!
As yet the poppies were not born
Between the blades of tender corn;
The last eggs had not hatched as yet,
Nor any bird forgot its mate.

I cannot tell you what it was;
But this I know: it did but pass.
It passed away with sunny May,
With all sweet things it passed away,
And left me old, and cold, and grey.

CHRISTINA ROSSETTI, 'May', from *Poetical Works* (1904)

The power of this near sonnet lies in its final reversal. May, in all its sweetness, fecundity and promise, is coupled, for the poet, with an intensely sad private event. An event which places her at a distance from her 'sunny' surroundings; which has left her, as she says, 'old, and cold, and grey'.

And so the poem's principle of articulation is antithesis.

Here, the speaker says, is May in all its beauty.

Here, she says, am I, bereft.

Something – she doesn't (or can't) vouchsafe what – amid the sweetness, has 'passed away'.

'May', we might think, and *may not*.

103

LEAR: No, no, no, no! Come, let's away to prison;
We two alone will sing like birds i' the cage:
When thou dost ask me blessing, I'll kneel down,
And ask of thee forgiveness: so we'll live,
And pray, and sing, and tell old tales, and laugh
At gilded butterflies, and hear poor rogues
Talk of court news; and we'll talk with them too,
Who loses and who wins; who's in, who's out;
And take upon's the mystery of things,
As if we were God's spies: and we'll wear out,
In a wall'd prison, packs and sets of great ones
That ebb and flow by the moon.
EDMUND: Take them away.
LEAR: Upon such sacrifices, my Cordelia,
The gods themselves throw incense. Have I caught thee?
He that parts us shall bring a brand from heaven,
And fire us hence like foxes. Wipe thine eyes;
The goujeres shall devour them, flesh and fell,
Ere they shall make us weep: we'll see 'em starve first.
Come.

WILLIAM SHAKESPEARE, *King Lear*, V.iii.8–26 (*c*.1605)

The poetry, as always, is in the poetry.

Desperate to see his life out with this daughter, Lear, the fantastic old man, offers images of their future. 'We two alone will sing like birds i' the cage'. And 'so', he says, again, 'we'll live, / And pray, and *sing*'. That second occurrence of the word is especially plaintive. As is the second instance of the word *out*. Time is running out for Lear. He is running out of options. And so he sings harder, imagines more vividly. 'Have I caught thee?' he asks. The answer he fears is 'No, no, no, no!'

104

Bare night is best. Bare earth is best. Bare, bare,
Except for our own houses, huddled low
Beneath the arches and their spangled air,
Beneath the rhapsodies of fire and fire,
Where the voice that is in us makes us a true response,
Where the voice that it is great within us rises up,
As we stand gazing at the rounded moon.

WALLACE STEVENS, from 'Evening without Angels' (1935)

Let us try to fathom this. Let us try to 'plummet' it, to take a word
from Herbert's 'Prayer' (No. 27). Let us consider what Stevens
means here as he confronts us with his repeated mumbling of
'Bare' and 'Bare'.

Many things are said to be 'bare' in Stevens. In his most famous
poem, 'The Anecdote of the Jar', the jar is 'gray and bare'. In 'The
Snow Man' we are given the 'wind / That is blowing in the same
bare place'. Here, now, 'Bare night is best. Bare earth is best.' Best
because in their bareness they are themselves.

What 'bare' indicates for Stevens is that which is not-human, that
which is outside and beyond human understanding, that which
has *not* been made over into human terms. Call it – as he does
here – the earth, or call it the universe. Call it the world, or call it
nature. Call it 'bare'.

But there, the poem says, is the problem. Once we call it anything
we have called it something. We have made it human. We have
given it a name. The word 'bare', so to speak, is 'bare', it cannot do
what it wants to do, it cannot say what the world is like outside
of thought.

Which would be a mere problem of words, were it not for the fact
that Stevens is telling us that we are caught within the language we
have for things, and that when we use words we are not describ-
ing those things but, to all intents and purposes, describing
ourselves.

We can ignore this fact, or like Empson we can 'let it go' (No. 84),
but we can't, as Stevens sees it, get away from it. The word is bare,
bare, bare.

And we have said too much.

105

From breakfast on through all the day
At home among my friends I stay;
But every night I go abroad
Afar into the land of Nod.

All by myself I have to go,
With none to tell me what to do –
All alone beside the streams
And up the mountain-sides of dreams.

The strangest things are there for me,
Both things to eat and things to see,
And many frightening sights abroad
Till morning in the land of Nod.

Try as I like to find the way,
I never can get back by day,
Nor can remember plain and clear
The curious music that I hear.

ROBERT LOUIS STEVENSON, 'The Land of Nod' (1885)

This children's poem – though what exactly is a children's poem
we're not at all sure that we know – encapsulates much of what
we have already talked of: adventure, mountains, streams and
food.

The poem's own little encapsulation occurs in the final line, in that
phrase 'curious music', a music that cannot be remembered 'plain
and clear'. In this the poem recalls George Herbert, of course
(No. 27), and William James (No. 31). And, uncannily, André
Breton:

106

One evening, therefore, before I fell asleep, I perceived so clearly articulated that it was impossible to change a word, but nonetheless removed from the sound of any voice, a rather strange phrase which came to me without any apparent relationship to the events in which, my consciousness agrees, I was then involved, a phrase which seemed to me insistent, a phrase, if I may be so bold, *which was knocking at the window*. I took cursory note of it and prepared to move on when its organic character caught my attention. Actually, this phrase astonished me: unfortunately I cannot remember it exactly, but it was something like: "There is a man cut in two by the window," but there could be no question of ambiguity, accompanied as it was by the faint visual image of a man cut half way up by a window perpendicular to the axis of his body. Beyond the slightest shadow of a doubt, what I saw was the simple reconstruction in space of a man leaning out a window. But this window having shifted with the man, I realized that I was dealing with an image of a fairly rare sort, and all I could think of was to incorporate it into my material for poetic construction.

ANDRÉ BRETON, 'Manifesto of Surrealism' (1924), tr. Richard Seaver and Helen R. Lane

Breton cannot remember exactly his astonishing phrase, but he incorporates it nonetheless into his material for 'poetic construction', and in so doing comes up with an even more astonishing phrase to describe the effect of the first astonishing phrase, '*which was knocking at the window*'.

Nothing ventured, nothing et cetera.

(And we are back here, note, in Robert Louis Stevenson's Land of Nod – the tap at the window.)

107

The sacredness which attaches to the act of creation,—
the act of thought,—is instantly transferred to the record.
The poet chanting, was felt to be a divine man. Hence-
forth the chant is divine also. The writer was a just and
wise spirit. Henceforward it is settled, the book is perfect;
as love of the hero corrupts into a worship of his statue.
Instantly, the book becomes noxious. The guide is a
tyrant.

RALPH WALDO EMERSON, 'The American Scholar' (1837)

Worship not the statue.

Worship not the book.

The book 'settled' becomes 'noxious'.

The guide is a tyrant.

108

Luxury, then, is a way of
being ignorant, comfortably
An approach to the open market
of least information. Where theories
can thrive, under heavy tarpaulins
without being cracked by ideas.

(I have not seen the earth for years
and think now possibly "dirt" is
negative, positive, but clearly
social. I cannot plant a seed, cannot
recognize the root with clearer dent
than indifference. Though I eat
and shit as a natural man. (Getting up
from the desk to secure a turkey sandwich
and answer the phone: the poem undone
undone by my station, by my station
and the bad words of Newark.) Raised up
to the breech, we seek to fill for this
crumbling century. The darkness of love,
in whose sweating memory all error is forced.

Undone by the logic of any specific death. (Old gentlemen
who still follow fires, tho are quieter
and less punctual. It is a polite truth
we are left with. Who are you? What are you
saying? Something to be dealt with, as easily.
The noxious game of reason, saying, "No, No,
you cannot feel," like my dead lecturer
lamenting thru gipsies his fast suicide.

LEROI JONES/AMIRI BARAKA, 'Political Poem' (1964)

The truth is not polite.

Luxury is noxious.

The only option, as Jones/Baraka rightly says, is 'being cracked by ideas'.

109

I spent the next two weeks in a passionate frenzy of
reading and learning. I scarcely left my room, I ate my
meals standing up so as not to waste time, I studied
unceasingly, without a break, almost without sleep. I was
like that prince in the Oriental fairy-tale who, removing
seal after seal from the doors of locked chambers, finds
more and more jewels and precious stones piled in each
room and makes his way with increasing avidity through
them all, eager to reach the last. In just the same way I
left one book to plunge into another, intoxicated by each
of them, never sated by any: my impetuosity had moved
on to intellectual concerns. I had a first glimmering of the
trackless expanses of the world of the mind, which I
found as seductive as the adventures of city life had been,
but at the same time I felt a boyish fear that I would not
be up to it, so I economized on sleep, on pleasures, on
conversation and any form of diversion merely so that I
could make full use of my time, which I had never felt so
valuable before. But what most inflamed my diligence
was vanity, a wish to come up to my teacher's expectations,
not to disappoint his confidence, to win a smile of
approval, I wanted him to be conscious of me as I was
conscious of him. Every fleeting occasion was a test; I
was constantly spurring my clumsy but now curiously
inspired mind on to impress and surprise him; if he
mentioned an author with whom I was unfamiliar during
a lecture, I would go in search of the writer's works that
very afternoon, so that next day I could show off by
parading my knowledge in the class discussion. A wish
uttered in passing which the others scarcely noticed was
transformed in my mind into an order; in this way a
casual condemnation of the way students were always
smoking was enough for me to throw away my lighted
cigarette at once, and give up the habit he deplored
at once and for ever. His words, like an evangelist's,
bestowed grace and were binding on me too; I was always
on the qui vive, attentive and intent upon greedily

snapping up every chance remark he happened to drop. I seized on every word, every gesture, and when I came home I bent my mind entirely to the passionate recapitulation and memorizing of what I had heard; my impatient ardour felt that he alone was my guide, and all the other students merely enemies whom my aspiring will urged itself to outstrip and out-perform.

STEFAN ZWEIG, *Confusion* (1927), tr. Anthea Bell

Much of this we would not discourage, except for eating 'standing up'; also 'intoxicated', 'seductive', 'vanity', 'evangelist's', as well as 'bestowed', 'grace', 'and', 'were', 'binding', 'on', 'me'. A 'frenzy of reading and learning', on the other hand, we positively endorse, as we do smoking, with none of the usual provisos.

110

I was just going, for example, to have given you the great outlines of my uncle Toby's most whimsical character;— when my aunt Dinah and the coachman came across us, and led us a vagary some millions of miles into the very heart of the planetary system: Notwithstanding all this you perceive that the drawing of my uncle Toby's character went on gently all the time;—not the great contours of it,—that was impossible,—but some familiar strokes and faint designations of it, were here and there touched in, as we went along, so that you are much better acquainted with my uncle Toby now than you was before.

By this contrivance the machinery of my work is of a species by itself; two contrary motions are introduced into it, and reconciled, which were thought to be at variance with each other. In a word, my work is digressive, and it is progressive, too,—and at the same time. [...]

Digressions, incontestably, are the sunshine;—they are the life, the soul of reading.

LAURENCE STERNE, *Tristram Shandy*, Volume 1, Chapter 22 (1759–67)

digress v. leave the main subject temporarily in speech or writing. [Origin C16: from L. *digress-*, *digredi* step away, from *di-* 'aside', + *gradi* to walk.]

Witness: 'I found a ball of grass among the hay / And progged it as I passed and went away' (No. 89).

Witness also: 'I was trotting along and suddenly / it started raining and snowing / and you said it was hailing / but hailing hits you on the head' (No. 100).

Or again: 'Finished a bottle of coke, and my last cigarette, before retiring, / a blind man stumbles out, tapping his cane loudly' (No. 92).

Digressed, progged, trotted along and stumbled out. Or, as the etymology suggests, and as Frank O'Hara demonstrates elsewhere, *stepped away:*

It's my lunch hour, so I go
for a walk among the hum-colored
cabs. First, down the sidewalk
where laborers feed their dirty
glistening torsos sandwiches
and Coca-Cola, with yellow helmets
on.
('A Step Away From Them', 1956)

A poem, by this way of thinking, is nothing more and nothing less
– is precisely, in fact – a stepping away, a digression, from what
might seem like the main subject at hand. Here the main subject is
work, but it's the poet's lunch hour and so he steps away into the
New York street, where it's all happening, where life (as opposed
to work) is going on. 'Digressions incontestably,' Sterne asserts,
'are the sunshine;—they are the life, the soul of reading.' In digres-
sion, the thought is, lies discovery, the poet's stumbling on.

As for 'the main subject [...] in speech and writing' – if you would
like, and if you have not already done so – see Jacques Derrida, *Of
Grammatology*, in which the whole of Western philosophy is shown
to be constructed upon the false subordination of the latter
(writing) to the former (speech).

111

In all judgements by which we describe anything as beautiful we tolerate no one else being of a different opinion, and in taking up this position we do not rest our judgement upon concepts, but only on our feeling. Accordingly we introduce this fundamental feeling not as a private feeling, but as a public sense. Now, for this purpose, experience cannot be made the ground of this common sense, for the latter is invoked to justify judgements containing an 'ought'. The assertion is not that every one *will* fall in with our judgement, but rather that every one *ought* to agree with it. Here I put forward my judgement of taste as an example of the judgement of common sense, and attribute to it on that account *exemplary* validity.

IMMANUEL KANT, *The Critique of Judgement* (1790), tr. James Creed Meredith

Ask yourself, reader, is it beautiful?

Not, in my opinion is it beautiful?

Nor, in somebody else's opinion might it be thought beautiful?

Ask yourself, reader, is it beautiful?

I am not a painter, I am a poet.
Why? I think I would rather be
a painter, but I am not. Well,

for instance, Mike Goldberg
is starting a painting. I drop in.
"Sit down and have a drink" he
says. I drink; we drink. I look
up. "You have SARDINES in it."
"Yes, it needed something there."
"Oh." I go and the days go by
and I drop in again. The painting
is going on, and I go, and the days
go by. I drop in. The painting is
finished. "Where's SARDINES?"
All that's left is just
letters, "It was too much," Mike says.

But me? One day I am thinking of
a color: orange. I write a line
about orange. Pretty soon it is a
whole page of words, not lines.
Then another page. There should be
so much more, not of orange, of
words, of how terrible orange is
and life. Days go by. It is even in
prose, I am a real poet. My poem
is finished and I haven't mentioned
orange yet. It's twelve poems, I call
it ORANGES. And one day in a gallery
I see Mike's painting, called SARDINES.

FRANK O'HARA, 'Why I am not a painter' (1956)

'Ut pictura poesis' said Horace – a poem is like a painting. O'Hara, many of whose friends were painters, and who would, in so many ways, really rather have been a painter, wants to insist on a distinction. 'I go and the days go by / and I drop in again. The painting / is going on, and I go, and the days / go by.' There's the distinction. The days go by and O'Hara records them going by,

and as he does so he records the making of the painting. The painting, on the other hand, evolves by putting its past behind it. 'The painting is / finished. "Where's SARDINES?"'

And so there you have it: a poem is not like a painting.

A poem lives through time.

A painting, temporally speaking, is fixed.

'I look / at bargains in wristwatches,' O'Hara says in 'A Step Away From Them', conscious always of the need to tell the time.

Telling the time is what a poem does. Remember Thomas Hardy (No. 51).

113 You can't say it that way any more.
Bothered about beauty you have to
Come out into the open, into a clearing,
And rest. Certainly whatever funny happens to you
Is OK. To demand more than this would be strange
Of you, you who have so many lovers,
People who look up to you and are willing
To do things for you, but you think
It's not right, that if they really knew you ...
So much for self-analysis. Now,
About what to put in your poem-painting:
Flowers are always nice, particularly delphinium.
Names of boys you once knew and their sleds,
Skyrockets are good—do they still exist?
There are a lot of other things of the same quality
As those I've mentioned. Now one must
Find a few important words, and a lot of low-keyed,
Dull-sounding ones. She approached me
About buying her desk. Suddenly the street was
Bananas and the clangor of Japanese instruments.
Humdrum testaments were scattered around. His head
Locked into mine. We were a seesaw. Something
Ought to be written about how this affects
You when you write poetry:
The extreme austerity of an almost empty mind
Colliding with the lush, Rousseau-like foliage of its desire
    to communicate
Something between breaths, if only for the sake
Of others and their desire to understand you and desert you
For other centres of communication, so that understanding
May begin, and in doing so be undone.

JOHN ASHBERY, 'And *Ut Pictura Poesis* Is Her Name' (1977)

On the other hand, maybe once it was; maybe a poem was like a
painting; or maybe, at least, it seemed to be so. But the point is, so
John Ashbery says – and he too had many friends who were
painters, many of the same friends as Frank O'Hara in fact – that
'You can't say it that way any more'.

But Ashbery's distinction isn't a matter of time, it's a matter of materials. What does it mean, he wonders, to put skyrockets and delphinium in your poem? It doesn't mean what it meant to the painter. What it means is 'skyrockets' and 'delphinium'.

A poem, Ashbery feels obliged to point out, is an arrangement of words.

'Now one must / Find a few important words, and a lot of low-keyed, / Dull-sounding ones.' Which is true, though to some it sounds reductive.

It is not reductive. How else does a poem get written?

A poem is not like a painting.

There's no paint.

114

The chief use of the 'meaning' of a poem, in the ordinary sense, may be [...] to satisfy one habit of the reader, to keep his mind diverted and quiet, while the poem does its work upon him; much as the imaginary burglar is always provided with a bit of nice meat for the house-dog.

T.S. ELIOT, 'The Use of Poetry and the Use of Criticism' (1933)

Which makes it all sound a bit insidious, doesn't it, a little bit cloak and dagger?

But then it is.

The meaning of the poem, as Eliot says, 'in the ordinary sense', is a decoy, and so the wrong question to ask of a poem is, what does it mean? The question to ask, rather, is does it *work*, where what that question means is, does it do the *work* of art?

Which work, we might remind you (see Nos. 1–113) is not necessarily at the level of reflection and category, but rather at the level of the particular.

'Suddenly the street was / Bananas and the clangor of Japanese instruments. / Humdrum testaments were scattered around.'

115 Break, break, break,
    On thy cold gray stones, O Sea!
And I would that my tongue could utter
    The thoughts that arise in me.

O well for the fisherman's boy,
    That he shouts with his sister at play!
O well for the sailor lad,
    That he sings in his boat on the bay!

And the stately ships go on
    To their haven under the hill;
But O for the touch of a vanished hand,
    And the sound of a voice that is still!

Break, break, break,
    At the foot of thy crags, O Sea!
But the tender grace of a day that is dead
    Will never come back to me.

ALFRED LORD TENNYSON, 'Break, Break, Break' (1842)

Here, in order to see how this poem works, we would offer a full definition of the word break. But the full definition is too long; one of the longest, you will notice, in the whole dictionary.

Why is that? Why so long a definition of so short and obvious a word?

Tennyson tells us why.

With each break of the waves – with each curling over and dissolving into foam – the further the speaker is broken from his past; where break means rupture, or severance, or disconnection: 'But O for the touch of a vanished hand'.

'I write poems,' Philip Larkin once remarked, 'to preserve things I have seen/thought/felt (if I may so indicate a composite and complex experience) both for myself and for others, though I feel that my prime responsibility is to the experience itself, which I am trying to keep from oblivion for its own sake. Why I should do this I have no idea, but I think that the impulse to preserve lies at the bottom of all art.'

'I look / at bargains in wristwatches,' O'Hara wrote, in 'A Step Away From Them'.

Such poets write because of the *break*, because as they proceed things get broken. Because 'the tender grace of a day that is dead / Will never come back to me'.

Everything breaks.

116

My name ys Parott, a byrde of Paradyse,
By Nature devysed of a wonderowus kynde,
Deyntely dyetyd with dyvers delycate spyce,
Tyll Eufrates, that flodde, dryvythe me into Ynde,
Where men of that contre by fortune me fynde,
And send me to greate ladyes of estate;
Then Parot moste have an almon or a date.

A cage curyowsly carven, with sylver pynne,
Properly payntyd to be my coverture;
A myrrour of glasse, that I may tote therin;
These maydens full meryly with many a dyvers flowur
Fresshely they dresse and make swete my bowur,
With, 'Speke, Parott, I pray yow,' full cureteslye they sey,
'Parott ys a goodlye byrde and a pratye popagay.'

JOHN SKELTON, 'Speke, Parott', ll.1–14 (c.1325)

A poem, it has been established, you may recall, is not like a painting.

The question remains, is it like a piece of music?

It is recommended that you speak 'Speke, Parott' aloud, and in the process that you consider its alliteration: 'These maydens full meryly with many a dyvers flowur'. And then, having got your tongue around it, having enunciated the music of the poem's consonants, you might want to consider the parrot's question: in speech, who is it – or what Is It – that speaks?

For Skelton the question was political. He wrote 'Speke, Parott' over many years, and, as far as its fragments are understood, meant It as a satire on courtly power. Who speaks, he wondered, when a courtier speaks? Who speaks, the poem continues to ask, when we are speaking?

Here, in the music of the poem, the sounds of the language speak.

117

Be not afeard: the isle is full of noises,
Sounds and sweet airs, that give delight, and hurt not.
Sometimes a thousand twangling instruments
Will hum about mine ears; and sometimes voices,
That, if I then had wak'd after long sleep,
Will make me sleep again: and then, in dreaming,
The clouds methought would open and show riches
Ready to drop upon me; that, when I wak'd
I cried to dream again.

WILLIAM SHAKESPEARE, *The Tempest*, III.ii.147–155 (1611)

Here Caliban speaks, who, before Prospero taught him, 'wouldst gabble like / A thing most brutish'. But taught him for what? Prospero taught Caliban language so as to put him to use. Whereupon, of course, Caliban got ideas above his station. In which situation there is a whole history of struggle and oppression; and, by the by, a whole defence of poetry.

A poem, it is to be emphasized, is an arrangement of words which gives people ideas above their station.

Caliban, of course, speaks beautifully, and, as he speaks, shows himself equal to beauty: 'The clouds methought would open and show riches / Ready to drop upon me.' As evidence of which Shakespeare permits him the word twangling, being only the third recorded use of the word. 'Twangling' being, according to the *OED*, 'a twangling sound; a continuous or repeated resonant sound, usually lighter or thinner than a twang'.

Not a twang, but a twangling: Caliban's speech could hardly be more precise.

Caliban is the archetype of the dispossessed. He is the case for poetic language.

Let's start from the smallest particle of all, the syllable. It is the king and pin of versification, what rules and holds together the lines, the larger forms of a poem. I would suggest that verse here and in England dropped this secret from the late Elizabethans to Ezra Pound, lost it, in the sweetness of meter and rime, in a honey-head. (The syllable is one way to distinguish the original success of blank verse, and its falling off, with Milton.)

It is by their syllables that words juxtapose in beauty, by these particles of sound as clearly as by the sense of the words which they compose. In any given instance, because there is a choice of words, the choice, if a man is in there, will be, spontaneously, the obedience of his ear to the syllables. The fineness and the practice, lie here, at the minimum and source of speech.

> O western wynd, when wilt thou blow
> And the small rain down shall rain
> O Christ that my love were in my arms
> And I in my bed again

CHARLES OLSON, 'Projective Verse' (1950)

We agree: the syllable. Stop hearing the syllable and the language is lost. There, among the particles, is articulation, where to ar-tic-u-late is to speak fluently, but it is also to have – in the sense of a body – joints or jointed segments.

'The fineness and the practice, lie here, at the minimum and source of speech.' Petty details. Petty, petty details.

119

If you've ever been in a car
that was hit by a train
whang
(a tearing like metal shears)
flip   spin
            "Why I'm perfectly OK!"
this streaming blood
a euphoric sweat of thanksgiving
and later

a hunk of scrap iron
just there on the turnpike
for no reason
flies up and
whang
it goes on your new underneath
well, it's like you were thrown
grabbed by the scruff of the neck
head over heels into Proust's steamy cup
just another crumb
of scalloped cookie
odious and total memory
                        (of the cells, no doubt)
in prickle-green, speed-lashed
Massachusetts

JAMES SCHUYLER, 'Stun' (1969)

Nobody – 'whang' – handled the syllable as well as James Schuyler, a poet whose greatness is still not widely known (now you know).

And not just the onomatopoeic syllable – whang – but all syllables, always: 'of scalloped cookie', 'in prickle-green, speed-lashed / Massachusetts'. A Schuyler poem is an act of constant differentiation, one syllable after another; each part of the language heard, and sounded, for itself. But not just for itself, for the world, because in differentiating thoroughly between sounds, he presents a way of writing capable of differentiating between things.

Wallace Stevens helps here. Little, Stevens says, 'will appear to

have suffered more from the passage of time than the music of poetry', a fact which matters, as he sees it, because the poet's 'role is to help people live their lives. He has had immensely to do with giving life whatever savor it possesses.'

Schuyler 'savors' language – 'zip', as another poem goes, 'thud' – in order that he and others might better savour things. Which takes us back to 'twangling', which takes us back to 'Deyntely dyetyd', which takes us back to 'hey, ho', 'aye' and 'o', and 'fa fa fa fa fa fa fa fa fa fa', which takes us back, so Schuyler would understand it, to 'prickle-green, speed-lashed / Massachusetts'.

120

Poetry is a composition of words set to music. Most other definitions of it are indefensible, or metaphysical. The proportion or quality of the music may, and does, vary; but poetry withers and 'dries out' when it leaves music, or at least an imagined music, too far behind it.

EZRA POUND, 'Vers Libre and Arnold Dolmetsch' (1918)

Agreed, with a proviso. Never agree with Ezra Pound without a proviso. Even Ezra Pound didn't agree with Ezra Pound without a proviso:

'As regarding rhythm: to compose in sequence of the musical phrase, not in sequence of the metronome' ('Vorticism').

In which two modes, as any music teacher will be able to tell you, there is all the difference.

121 "First thou shalt come to the Sirens, the maids that
    enchant
All men that go on the sea who their island approach:
For whoso the sound of their song has unwittingly heard,
Never can he to his wife and children return
In his own native land, nor they in his coming have joy,
For the Sirens bewitch him, singing their musical strain
Where they lie in the mead, and around is a heap of the
    bones
Of mouldering men and of dead skin wasting away.
Drive thou past them and stop thy company's ears
With honey-sweet wax well-kneaded, lest any their song
May hear; but if thou thyself shouldst be minded to hear,
Hand and foot let thy comrades bind thee with cords
Upright in the mast-box, and fasten the ends to the mast,
That thou in the song of the Sirens mayst have thy delight.
But if then thou beseech thy companions the bonds to
    unloose,
Let them bring yet more and enwind thee the tighter in
    them."

[...]

'So charged I my comrades and warn'd them of all they
    should do,
And meanwhile our well-wrought galley had quickly
    arrived
At the isle of the Sirens, sped by the favouring breeze.
But the wind of a sudden was hush'd, and there fell on
    the ship
A windless calm, and the billows were lull'd by a God,
And straightway my company took in the sail of the ship
And stow'd it away in the hold and sate to their oars
And whiten'd the sea with the stroke of their well-polish'd
    blades.
But I with my sword divided a great roll of wax,
Cutting it small, and with strong hands kneaded it well;
And quickly it melted, constrain'd by the strength of my
    hands
And the hot beams of the Sun-god Hyperion.

And the ears of my men, each in order, I stopp'd with the
    wax,
And me they lash'd with a cord, both my hands and my
    feet,
Upright in the mast-box, and tied up the ends to the mast,
And themselves on the grey salt water smote with their
    oars.
But when now no further away than a voice might be
    heard,
We rowing at speed, the Sirens our vessel espied
As nearer it mov'd, and began their melodious song:
"Come hither, O pride of Achaea, Odysseus renown'd,
    And stay thy bark that our voice mayst hear
For never a sailor has pass'd in his black-painted ship
    Ere the honey-sweet strain of our voice he might hear;
And a gladder and wiser man he has gone on his way,
    For we know all the toils that the Trojans and ye
By the will of the Gods on the plains of Troyland endur'd,
    Yea, all on the fruitful earth that hereafter shall be."'

HOMER, *The Odyssey*, Book 12, ll.40–55, 166–192 (*c.*730BC), tr. S.O. Andrew

**There is no stronger reading of these lines than that offered by
Max Horkheimer and Theodor Adorno in 'The Concept of Enlight-
enment' (*Dialectic of Enlightenment: Philosophical Fragments*). Here,
they suggest, at the practical beginning of poetry, is all that might
be said about the relation of poetry to work. More than that, here,
at the practical beginning of poetry, poetry is understood in
fundamental opposition to work.**

**What the myth depicts is the 'comrades', who are in fact workers,
rowing grimly on, ears blocked against the beauty and implica-
tions of the sirens' song. What it depicts also, however, is Odysseus
– landowner and employer – subjecting himself to an even greater
discipline. It is not that he, as the poem's representative of
management culture, must not allow himself to hear the bland-
ishments of the sirens' song, which is to say the possibilities
for existence offered and contemplated by poetry. It is, instead,
that as such a figure he must train himself to *hear* such blandish-**

ments (possibilities) and also, at the same time, to *deny* them to himself.

The worker, in the face of beauty and possibility, must be rendered deaf.

The employer/director/landowner must, by contrast, be made resolute.

But what are those blandishments? What are the possibilities that Horkheimer and Adorno hear in the song of the sirens? What they hear, there, is the prospect of an existence unstructured by occupation, an existence in which consciousness and knowledge wash back and forth. An existence in which people don't have to steel themselves to perform a specific function. An existence, if one might say so, more fluidly and expansively human.

The message of the passage then?

Contrary to Circe, contrary perhaps even to Homer (who knows) – *listen* to the poem, the sound of the sirens singing.

The poem, that is, as opposed to money:

122　I listen to money singing. It's like looking down
　　　From long French windows at a provincial town,
　　The slums, the canal, the churches ornate and mad
　　　In the evening sun. It is intensely sad.

PHILIP LARKIN, from 'Money' (1973)

Note: not the smell of money; nor the colour of money. The *sound* of money: gold, silver, copper, paper. We all know that money talks. But Philip Larkin can hear it sing.

Money is a kind of poetry: they are both an IOU; a substitution; a fiction.

So why is it so intensely sad, the sound of money?

Because, so one might conjecture, time is money. Or to put it the other way around, money is time. And so if money sings, like the sirens, what it sings of is the way time has been spent. Money singing is the sound of time 'used up' (see also Heidegger, No. 43).

It is clear now:

Neither Honey nor
the honey bee is
to be mine again

SAPPHO, Fragment 146 (*c*.600BC), tr. Mary Bernard

**An epic is a poem containing history. A fragment is a part implying
a whole. (From, if we might say so, the Latin *frangere*, to break,
which takes us back, rightly enough, to Tennyson, No. 115.)**

All poems are fragments of sorts.

124 Witness:

Times Square

a furtive queen
            hurrying across a deserted thoroughfare
                                                at dawn

JOHN WIENERS, 'Times Square' (1970)

125

I once tore up a sapling to make myself a stick:
it clung to the earth, but I cut away its roots,
stripped off its twigs and bark;
a woman passing nodded her head as if to say, What a pity,
and I had no joy of the stick and threw it away.

CHARLES REZNIKOFF, *Jerusalem the Golden*, Section 65 (1934)

Jerusalem the Golden is a single poem consisting of a long series of numbered fragments, some of them linking directly to the fragments adjacent to them, some of them not. As a whole the poem recalls, among many other texts, the Old Testament, which is itself a long series of fragments – God himself, it seems, choosing to articulate himself in apparently disconnected bits.

Some of Reznikoff's fragments are in the nature of aphorisms, as in 'I once tore up a sapling to make myself a stick'. Here the aphorism tells us something about what happens when you take a thing out of its original context and fashion it into something else. It also tells us, in no uncertain terms, what to think about what other people think.

Perhaps you know the story about the old man and his young son travelling across the desert, leading a camel?

Someone passes them, coming in the opposite direction. 'Fools!' the stranger says. 'Why exhaust yourselves on your journey? Why not ride on the camel?' So the old man mounts the camel and rides upon it.

Then someone else passes them and says to the old man, 'Wretch! You shouldn't allow the young boy to walk in such heat!' So the old man dismounts and allows the young boy to ride the camel.

Then someone else passes by and says to the young boy, 'Ingrate! How dare you ride while your elder and better walks!' So the young boy dismounts from the camel, and with the old man they carry the camel across the desert.

126

The primary function of poetry, as of all the arts, is to make us more aware of ourselves and the world around us. I do not know if such increased awareness makes us more moral or more efficient. I hope not. I think it makes us more human, and I am quite certain it makes us more difficult to deceive.

W.H. AUDEN, from *The English Auden: Poems, Essays and Dramatic Writings, 1927–1939*, ed. Edward Mendelson (1977)

Personally, we remain easy to deceive.

So, presumably, poetry cannot be a truth serum.

127

As I in hoary winter's night stood shivering in the snow,
Surprised I was with sudden heat which made my heart
    to glow;
And lifting up a fearful eye to view what fire was near,
A pretty babe all burning bright did in the air appear;
Who, scorchèd with excessive heat, such floods of tears
    did shed
As though his floods should quench his flames which
    with his tears were fed.
"Alas," quoth he, "but newly born in fiery heats I fry,
Yet none approach to warm their hearts or feel my fire but I!
My faultless breast the furnace is, the fuel wounding
    thorns,
Love is the fire, and sighs the smoke, the ashes shame
    and scorns;
The fuel justice layeth on, and mercy blows the coals,
The metal in this furnace wrought are men's defilèd souls,
For which, as now on fire I am to work them to their good,
So will I melt into a bath to wash them in my blood."
With this he vanished out of sight and swiftly shrunk away,
And straight I callèd unto mind that it was Christmas day.

ROBERT SOUTHWELL, 'The Burning Babe' (1595)

It is recorded that Southwell (1561–95) was arrested and imprisoned by Queen Elizabeth I for administering the rites of the Catholic Church. 'Transferred to the gatehouse at Westminster, he was so abominably treated that his father petitioned Elizabeth that he might either be brought to trial and put to death, if found guilty, or removed in any case from "that filthy hole." Southwell was then lodged in the Tower, but he was not brought to trial until February 1595. There is little doubt that much of his poetry, none of which was published during his lifetime, was written in prison.' (*Encyclopedia Britannica*)

Once published, anonymously, *St Peter's Complaint with other Poems* was reprinted 13 times in 40 years, and Ben Jonson said he would have gladly destroyed many of his own poems to be able to say he had written 'The Burning Babe'.

This poem works in part by antithesis (heat/cold, flames/tears) but also – less obviously, but more devastatingly for that – by euphony, which is to say by its pleasing sounds.

Listen, for instance, to the vowel sounds of the opening line, which modulate to beautifully fluid effect. Or, more strikingly, perhaps, to the seventh line: '"Alas," quoth he, "but newly born in fiery heats I fry'.

Here, as in Homer, the music is a seduction, a distraction from the work really at hand.

Because, in fact, the poem is brutal, savagely brutal: the babe – Christ – is 'burning bright'; innocence has been put to death. But we don't hear this for a moment, not in its full harshness anyway. What we hear first is the music, the pleasing sounds.

The poem's brilliance lies in this disjunction, in the way that, as the babe speaks of being disregarded, so the reader is lulled into the same disregard. Until, that is, we are shocked out of our disregard, which, if we keep reading and thinking, we surely are. Until, so to speak, we don't hear any longer 'A pretty Babe all burning bright', but hear instead the force of *burning*, a 'Babe all burning', a *burning* babe.

And so in this case the poem does its work by first seducing us, and then by showing how appallingly we have been seduced. It endures because it can always speak to the reader who hears the music not the news. And the news, when it arrives in this poem – to use a word from Hopkins (No. 87) – 'explodes'.

128 They that have power to hurt and will do none,
  That do not do the thing they most do show,
Who, moving others, are themselves as stone,
  Unmovèd, cold, and to temptation slow;
They rightly do inherit heaven's graces,
  And husband nature's riches from expense;
They are lords and owners of their faces,
  Others but stewards of their excellence.
The summer's flower is to the summer sweet,
  Though to itself it only live and die;
But if that flower with base infection meet,
  The basest weed outbraves his dignity;
   For sweetest things turn sourest by their deeds;
   Lilies that fester smell far worse than weeds.

WILLIAM SHAKESPEARE, Sonnet 94 (1609)

For a commentary on this, see 'When I Buy Pictures':

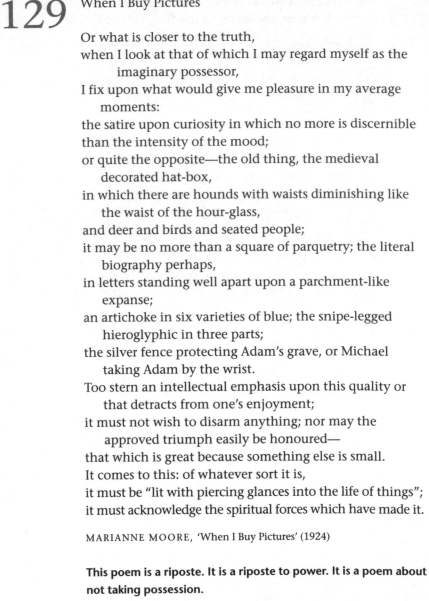

129 When I Buy Pictures

Or what is closer to the truth,
when I look at that of which I may regard myself as the
     imaginary possessor,
I fix upon what would give me pleasure in my average
     moments:
the satire upon curiosity in which no more is discernible
than the intensity of the mood;
or quite the opposite—the old thing, the medieval
     decorated hat-box,
in which there are hounds with waists diminishing like
     the waist of the hour-glass,
and deer and birds and seated people;
it may be no more than a square of parquetry; the literal
     biography perhaps,
in letters standing well apart upon a parchment-like
     expanse;
an artichoke in six varieties of blue; the snipe-legged
     hieroglyphic in three parts;
the silver fence protecting Adam's grave, or Michael
     taking Adam by the wrist.
Too stern an intellectual emphasis upon this quality or
     that detracts from one's enjoyment;
it must not wish to disarm anything; nor may the
     approved triumph easily be honoured—
that which is great because something else is small.
It comes to this: of whatever sort it is,
it must be "lit with piercing glances into the life of things";
it must acknowledge the spiritual forces which have made it.

MARIANNE MOORE, 'When I Buy Pictures' (1924)

This poem is a riposte. It is a riposte to power. It is a poem about
not taking possession.

The poet does not 'buy pictures'. Nor, as the qualifying second
lines state, does she want to. She wants a relation with the picture
she likes which does not involve control. Witness the art she stands
up for: 'it must not wish to disarm anything'. Marianne Moore is
against disarming. She eschews all the aspects of poetry that

might achieve such a disarming, all the aspects of poetry in which Southwell draped 'The Burning Babe' (No. 127).

This is why her poem is without metre, and it is why it is without cadence. She wants nothing that will over-ride the particulars of her work. Like Shakespeare, she admires those who 'have power to hurt and will do none'. More than Shakespeare she resists those aspects of language which lend themselves to power. She is a meticulous, unflinching acknowledger of things.

Because that's the word in this poem: 'acknowledge'. 'It must acknowledge'. Marianne Moore writes a poetry which refuses to hold sway.

The Enthusiast heartily – heartfeltfully – recommends Marianne Moore. She is that most valuable of creatures, a modest Modernist; a poet capable, in her wisdom, of valuing 'the average moments'.

She loved boxing, and cars, and circuses.

130

Poems very seldom consist of poetry and nothing else; and pleasure can be derived also from their other ingredients. I am convinced that most readers, when they think they are admiring poetry, are deceived by an inability to analyse their sensations, and that they are really admiring, not the poetry of the passage before them, but something else in it, which they like better than poetry.

A.E. HOUSMAN, 'The Name and Nature of Poetry' (1933)

Agreed: and the main other ingredient, we would suggest, is prose.

131

Life, friends, is boring. We must not say so.
After all, the sky flashes, the great sea yearns,
we ourselves flash and yearn,
and moreover my mother told me as a boy
(repeatingly) 'Ever to confess you're bored
means you have no

Inner Resources.' I conclude now I have no
inner resources, because I am heavy bored.
Peoples bore me,
literature bores me, especially great literature,
Henry bores me, with his plights & gripes
as bad as achilles,

who loves people and valiant art, which bores me.
And the tranquil hills, & gin, look like a drag
and somehow a dog
has taken itself & its tail considerably away
into mountains or sea or sky, leaving
behind: me, wag.

JOHN BERRYMAN, 'Dream Song 14' (1964)

John Berryman is a case in point. As a young man he was a most committed and intelligent reader of poetry, and for many years tried to write poems which consisted of 'poetry and nothing else'. He tried conventional form after conventional form, and gave himself over to their requirements and, sadly, their traditional subjects, and none of these poems, in all their poetical-ness, ever really worked. Even his best friends — Robert Lowell for instance – couldn't say they really worked. Berryman was missing the point. He couldn't see that pleasure can be derived from other ingredients.

And then he hit on a form of his own: the form of the Dream Song. And what he found in that form, that mis-shapen sonnet, was that he could speak about non-poetical things: about boredom, and dogs, and how everything looked like a drag. And so he carried on. He wrote hundreds of Dream Songs. Once he'd found his form, you might say, poetically speaking, Berryman never looked back.

As for boredom, try Coleridge:

132

All Nature seems at work. Slugs leave their lair—
The bees are stirring—birds are on the wing—
And Winter slumbering in the open air,
Wears on his smiling face a dream of Spring!
And I the while, the sole unbusy thing,
Nor honey make, nor pair, nor build, nor sing.

Yet well I ken the banks where amaranths blow,
Have traced the fount whence streams of nectar flow.
Bloom, O ye amaranths! Bloom for whom ye may,
For me ye bloom not! Glide, rich streams, away!
With lips unbrightened, wreathless brow, I stroll:
And would you learn the spells that drowse my soul?
Work without Hope draws nectar in a sieve,
And Hope without an object cannot live.

SAMUEL TAYLOR COLERIDGE, 'Work without Hope' (1828)

This poem is all upside down. A sonnet of sorts, the sestet comes before the octave. And is it winter, or is it spring? The poet is disorientated. He sees the activity of work all around him. But what, he wonders, is the poet's work?

And here, at least, he doesn't know. *Coleridge* doesn't know!

He thinks the poet's work is to produce that which consists only of poetry: 'of lips unbrightened', of 'wreathless brow', of 'amaranths'. This is poetry without purpose, language, as the poem seems honest enough to admit, without object. It is an example of poetry at its most redundant.

On the other hand:

133

Here, you see, are two kinds of work – one good, the other bad; one not far removed from a blessing, a lightening of life; the other a mere curse, a burden to life.

What is the difference between them, then? This one has hope in it, the other has not. It is manly to do the one kind of work, and manly also to refuse to do the other.

What is the nature of the hope which, when it is present in work, makes it worth doing?

It is threefold, I think – hope of rest, hope of product, hope of pleasure in the work itself; and hope of these also in some abundance and of good quality; rest enough and good enough to be worth having; product worth having by one who is neither a fool nor an ascetic; pleasure enough for all of us to be conscious of it while we are at work; not a mere habit, the loss of which we shall feel as a fidgety man feels the loss of the bit of string he fidgets with.

WILLIAM MORRIS, *Useful Work Versus Useless Toil* (1855)

The question is, does the *work* have hope in it?

Hope is a condition of the good work.

Equally:

134

That art that matters to us—which moves the heart, or revives the soul, or delights the senses, or offers courage for living, however we choose to describe the experience —that work is received by us as a gift is received. Even if we have paid a fee at the door of the museum or concert hall, when we are touched by a work of art something comes to us which has nothing to do with the price. I went to see a landscape painter's works, and that evening, walking among pine trees near my home, I could see the shapes and colors I had not seen the day before. The spirit of an artist's gifts can wake our own. The work appeals, as Joseph Conrad says, to a part of our being which is itself a gift and not an acquisition. Our sense of harmony can hear the harmonies that Mozart heard. We may not have the power to profess our gifts as the artist does, and yet we come to recognize, and in a sense to receive, the endowments of being through the agency of his creation. We feel fortunate, even redeemed. The daily commerce of our lives—"sugar for sugar and salt for salt," as the blues singers say—proceeds at its own constant level, but a gift revives the soul. When we are moved by art we are grateful that the artist lived, grateful that he labored in the service of his gifts.

LEWIS HYDE, *The Gift: Imagination and the Erotic Life of Property* (1979)

Which is what we were looking to say earlier – much earlier – about the closing down of possibility, about shopping and working, "sugar for sugar and salt for salt". Against such limited possibilities are the things, as Lewis Hyde brilliantly puts it, which offer 'courage for living'. That which, even if we have paid a fee for it, 'has nothing to do with the price'.

'I listen to money singing,' says Larkin, and 'It is intensely sad' (No. 122).

'Lana Turner we love you,' says O'Hara, 'get up' (No. 100).

135 The rhyme and uniformity of perfect poems show the free growth of metrical laws and bud from them as unerringly and loosely as lilacs or roses on a bush, and take shapes as compact as the shapes of chestnuts and oranges and melons and pears, and shed the perfume impalpable to form. The fluency and ornaments of the finest poems or music or orations or recitations are not independent but dependent. All beauty comes from beautiful blood and a beautiful brain. If the greatnesses are in conjunction in a man or a woman it is enough .... the fact will prevail through the universe .... but the gaggery and gilt of a million years will not prevail. Who troubles himself about his ornaments or fluency is lost. This is what you shall do: Love the earth and sun and animals, despise riches, give alms to every one that asks, stand up for the stupid and crazy, devote your income and labor to others, hate tyrants, argue not concerning God, have patience and indulgence toward the people, take off your hat to nothing known or unknown or to any man or number of men, go freely with powerful uneducated persons and with the young and with the mothers of families, read these leaves in the open air every season of every year of your life, re-examine all you have been told at school or church or in any book, dismiss whatever insults your own soul, and your very flesh shall be a great poem and have the richest fluency not only in its words but in the silent lines of its lips and face and between the lashes of your eyes and in every motion and joint of your body .... The poet shall not spend his time in unneeded work. He shall know that the ground is always ready plowed and manured .... others may not know it but he shall. He shall go directly to the creation. His trust shall master the trust of everything he touches .... and shall master all attachment.

WALT WHITMAN, from the Preface to the 1855 edition of *Leaves of Grass*

Not much to disagree with here, although surely it's a bit rich – a bit poor – of Whitman to propose poems as 'compact as the shapes of chestnuts and oranges and melons and pears'; Whitman –

Whitman! – Whitman, that is, who needed for his expression a whole prairie of leaves of grass.

What should be emphasized, though, is 'unneeded work', because that goes to the heart of him. 'He', by which he means the poet, 'shall go directly to the creation.' These two statements are linked to the matter of 'ornaments', which should be not be 'independent but dependent'. And all of this anticipates Ezra Pound when he insisted, in 'A Retrospect', on 'Direct treatment of the "thing," whether subjective or objective'.

Directness, Whitman understood in the middle of the 19th century, was where poetry was headed. Which is to say that the poet's work did not consist in establishing his credentials, did not consist in ornamentation, did not consist in perfecting this metaphor or that simile.

What it had to consist of, rather, was a direct address, a clear articulation of its object. Between people and people and between people and things, the poet's object was 'attachment'. Or as he calls it elsewhere, 'adhesion'. Whitman wanted desperately for the poem to 'adhere'.

Not to put too grand a construction upon it, but as America slipped towards civil war, Whitman wanted to keep its citizenship from falling apart. And so he proposes himself as that to which people might attach, not least in his love poems, such as this from 1860, 'Once I Pass'd through a Populous City':

> Once I pass'd through a populous city imprinting my brain
> for future use with its shows, architectures, customs,
> traditions,
> Yet now of all that city I remember only a woman I casually
> met there who detain'd me for love of me,
> Day by day and night by night we were together—all else
> has long been forgotten by me,
> I remember I say only that woman who passionately clung to me,
> Again we wander, we love, we separate again,
> Again she holds me by the hand, I must not go,
> I see her close beside me with the silent lips sad and
> tremulous.

Not, it must be said, that everybody clung to Whitman:

To become adopted as a national poet, it is not enough to discard everything in particular, and to accept everything in general, to amass crudity upon crudity, to discharge the undigested contents of your blotting-book into the lap of the public. You must respect the public which you address; for it has taste, if you have not. It delights in the grand, the heroic, and the masculine; but it delights to see these conceptions cast into worthy form. It is indifferent to brute sublimity. It will never do for you to thrust your hands into your pockets and cry out that, as the research of form is an intolerable bore, the shortest and most economical way for the public to embrace its idols —for the nation to realize its genius—is in your own person. [...] It is not enough to be rude, lugubrious, and grim. You must also be serious. You must forget yourself in your ideas. Your personal qualities—the vigour of your temperament, the manly independence of your nature, the tenderness of your heart—these facts are impertinent. You must be possessed, and you must strive to possess your possession. If in your striving you break into divine eloquence, then you are a poet.

HENRY JAMES, review of Walt Whitman's *Drum-Taps*, in *The Nation*, 16 November 1865

Reviews of Whitman's poetry were – how can one put it? – *varied*.

The ones he wrote himself, and published anonymously, on the appearance of the first edition of *Leaves of Grass* were, needless to say, glowing. (And really, as an innovator in the field of literary publicity, Whitman has hardly been bettered since. Not for him a few appearances at festivals and a desultory book signing. Instead, an anonymous self-assertion that, though readers might not see it yet, his work was great. And why not? He was ahead of his time, as all great poets are ahead of their time. If he wasn't to explain himself to people then who would, Henry James?)

Not so glowing, though, as the letter Ralph Waldo Emerson wrote him on receiving his book.

'I greet you,' Emerson wrote, 'at the beginning of a great career, which yet must have had a long foreground somewhere, for such a start.'

And then there was James, who manages both to get the point and, at the same time, miss it entirely. Whitman *did* 'amass crudity upon crudity', and he did insist on 'vigour' and 'tenderness'. He *was* making a direct appeal to the public. He was not, however – absolutely not it should be noticed – discarding everything in particular. 'Song of Myself', in all its itemizing, is a masterpiece of the particular.

What James most singularly fails to appreciate, however, is the nature of Whitman's *address*.

Whitman addressed himself to the present – to his comrades – but also to the future. His address to the present was simplified. His address to the future was complex and rich.

What it means to 'strive to possess your possession' we cannot say. We suspect, though, that 'To become adopted as a national poet' it is a necessary condition to have a care for the future.

It's a risk.

137

I met a traveller from an antique land
Who said: Two vast and trunkless legs of stone
Stand in the desert…Near them, on the sand,
Half sunk, a shattered visage lies, whose frown,
And wrinkled lip, and sneer of cold command,
Tell that its sculptor well those passions read
Which yet survive, stamped on these lifeless things,
The hand that mocked them, and the heart that fed:
And on the pedestal these words appear:
'My name is Ozymandias, king of kings:
Look on my works, ye Mighty, and despair!'
Nothing beside remains. Round the decay
Of that colossal wreck, boundless and bare
The lone and level sands stretch far away.

PERCY BYSSHE SHELLEY, 'Ozymandias' (1818)

Shelley too took risks.

Shelley too addressed the future.

One might say, in fact, that the future was Shelley's province.

The poet, as he tells it in *A Defence of Poetry* (where he is not, alas, future-minded enough to notice that such a creature might not be a man), 'not only beholds intensely the present as it is, and discovers those laws according to which present things ought to be ordered, but he beholds the future in the present, and his thoughts are the germs of the flower and the fruit of latest time'.

'Ozymandias' opens with 'a traveller from an antique land'. It ends as, 'boundless and bare / The lone and level sands stretch far away'. The poem, one might think, is an act of clearing. Unable directly to influence the past and the present, the poem projects the reader into the future. The word for the future is 'boundless' – boundless, and, because as yet unwritten, 'bare'.

Equally, of course, the word might be 'damned':

138

non peccat, quaecumque potest peccasse negare,
solaque famosam culpa professa facit.

(AMORES, III, XIV)

I love my work and my children. God
Is distant, difficult. Things happen.
Too near the ancient troughs of blood
Innocence is no earthly weapon.

I have learned one thing: not to look down
So much upon the damned. They, in their sphere,
Harmonize strangely with the divine
Love. I, in mine, celebrate the love-choir.

GEOFFREY HILL, 'Ovid in the Third Reich' (1968)

The epigraph, from elegy xiv of the third of Ovid's books of love poems, translated: 'She who can deny having sinned does not sin, and only the fault confessed makes her notorious.'

Ovid's elegy is painfully ironic. It asks that his mistress should not tell him of her infidelities because, so to speak, what he doesn't know can't hurt him. The elegy begins happily enough, mocking his mistress's antics. It ends as a desperate act of self-denial. He knows what he knows, he would just rather his mistress didn't tell him what he knows. That way, at least, he can pretend that the things she does don't happen.

'Things happen.'

Geoffrey Hill's poem is spoken by Ovid – it is a dramatic monologue. The speaker in a dramatic monologue is a masque, or, to use Ezra Pound's term, a persona. The persona can provide a way of addressing a subject that it is difficult, perhaps even impossible, to address directly.

The key sentence: 'I have learned one thing: not to look down / So much upon the damned.' Does this mean, as perhaps it first seems to, that Ovid cannot bring himself to look down upon those, the Jews, damned by the Third Reich? This would seem, unavoidably, to be one of the sentence's meanings. There are the victims of the Holocaust, in the 'troughs of blood'. Ovid, too near to the event, has learned to stop himself looking down upon them.

But remember Empson: 'The machinations of ambiguity are among the very roots of poetry' (see No. 97). And then consider that there, in that phrase 'the damned', it is possible – necessary one might say – to identify not just the victims of the Holocaust but the perpetrators too. If anybody in this circumstance is damned it is surely the Nazis. Which makes it, then, a still more disturbing question: what does it mean here, 'not to look down / So much upon the damned'.

What it must partly mean is that the speaker doesn't want to see what the Nazis are doing, would like, rather, as with the speaker of Ovid's elegy, not to know. Or worse still, he would like not to be reminded, or told, of what he does know.

But then, having remembered Empson, one has to remember him again – and keep remembering him – because real ambiguity, however much you might settle it, doesn't ever settle down.

What the line must also mean, then, following from the situation of the elegy, is that the speaker has learned not to look down so much upon the damned because he doesn't feel in a position to do so; because 'Things happen' and he knows they happen and because, in knowing they happen, he does nothing to stop them. He – the speaker, Ovid – doesn't look down on the Nazis not because he doesn't disapprove – how could he not disapprove? – but because disapproval isn't sufficient. Because in some sense he is complicit, because in some sense he is culpable. We know terrible things happen, and could try to prevent them. We don't. We let them pass. What does it mean to disapprove?

But what of love? Must it not be celebrated in spite of all?

'Ovid in the Third Reich' is a dense field of meaning. Consider, for instance, the poem's half rhymes: 'happen' and 'weapon', 'divine' and 'down'. Through the allusion of its epigraph it creates a complex of views and viewpoints. One of its questions, to which it barely manages an answer, is: what is love? Or to be more precise, where the world is rotten, can love be maintained?

But the poem's questions on this subject go deeper still. See that the damned, in the penultimate sentence, 'Harmonize strangely with the divine / Love'. Which is to say that the damned and the innocent are somehow not distinguishable. Maybe this says something about distance. Maybe, from a certain distance, the perpetrator and the victim don't look so different. Maybe – in some horribly uneasy and ambiguous sense – they all look the same to God.

Or maybe what is at issue here is words. Maybe there are some circumstances – this would surely be one of them – when the language we have available is insufficient, when the terms of judgement – 'damned', 'innocence' – are seen to fail.

And so what we find perhaps, where least we wanted to find it, is that there, in the 'ancient troughs of blood', ambiguity is more than ever to be found at the root.

This we don't want to know.

It is a profoundly troubling thought.

Whichever way you look at it.

Something is rotten in the state of Denmark.

WILLIAM SHAKESPEARE, *Hamlet*, I.iv.90 (1600–01)

In the absence, yet, of overwhelming motive – a faintly suspicious death, an over-hasty marriage, but nothing quite so decisive as to compel action – Marcellus, one of the King's guard, and a spectator on events, offers up the most telling comment on the action that defines the play.

The state, here, is The State, the political apparatus of the nation; a nation on heightened alert against a political invader. The state is also the *state*, the condition of Denmark, the prevailing mentality, the population's emotional health. Of which Hamlet is the symptom. He is in no fit state. He is driven to action, but he can't act. He reflects, and as he questions himself, he scrutinizes his own and everybody else's moves. Hamlet's state – Denmark's – is a state of surveillance.

The point is that everybody is a spy.

Polonius hires young men to spy on Laertes. He spies on Hamlet and Ophelia. He dies spying on Hamlet and the Queen. Gertrude and Claudius hire Rosencrantz and Guildenstern to spy on Hamlet, but Hamlet is so used to the operation that he spots them a mile off. Spying is habitual. Neither Gertrude nor Ophelia raises an eyebrow when asked to accede to this requirement. Hamlet stages a play in order to spy on the King. He feigns madness that he might spy on everybody else, but even as he does so he is wracked with doubt.

Caught in a web of surveillance, Hamlet's tragedy is that he spies on himself – checks himself, admonishes himself, inspects his motivations. 'Something,' as Marcellus shrewdly observes, 'is rotten in the state of Denmark.' Here is a state in which there is no trust, and in which everybody, as a consequence, is acting out their part. The play is a guide to the language and emotion of the paranoid state. Hamlet, Prince of Denmark, it seems safe to say, is not an enthusiast.

140

A sight in camp in the daybreak gray and dim,
As from my tent I emerge so early sleepless,
As slow I walk in the cool fresh air the path near by the
    hospital tent,
Three forms I see on stretchers lying, brought out there
    untended lying,
Over each the blanket spread, ample brownish woollen
    blanket,
Gray and heavy blanket, folding, covering all.

Curious I halt and silent stand,
Then with light fingers I from the face of the nearest the
    first just lift the blanket;
Who are you elderly man so gaunt and grim, with well-
    gray'd hair, and flesh all sunken about the eyes?
Who are you my dear comrade?
Then to the second I step—and who are you my child
    and darling

Who are you sweet boy with cheeks yet blooming?

Then to the third—a face nor child nor old, very calm, as
    of beautiful yellow-white ivory;
Young man I think I know you—I think this face is the
    face of the Christ himself,
Dead and divine and brother of all, and here again he lies.

WALT WHITMAN, 'A Sight in Camp in the Daybreak Gray and Dim' (1865)

Whitman wrote this poem from the battlefields of the American civil
war. It is one of those poems James was reviewing when he sug-
gested that Whitman discarded 'everything in particular' (No. 136).

But here is the particular: the poet lifts the blanket, 'Gray and
heavy blanket, folding, covering all'.

'And who are you my child and darling // Who are you sweet boy
with cheeks yet blooming?'

In Whitman, as in Hill, writing from the field of death, *in* death
the victim harmonizes 'strangely with the divine'.

Ends

141

By heaven, man, we are turned round and round in this world, like yonder windlass, and Fate is the handspike. And all the time, lo! that smiling sky, and this unsounded sea! Look! see yon Albicore! who put it into him to chase and fang that flying-fish? Where do murderers go, man! Who's to doom, when the judge himself is dragged to the bar? But it is a mild, mild wind, and a mild looking sky; and the air smells now, as if it blew from a far-away meadow; they have been making hay somewhere under the slopes of the Andes, Starbuck, and the mowers are sleeping among the new-mown hay. Sleeping? Aye, toil we how we may, we all sleep at last on the field. Sleep? Aye, and rust amid greenness; as last year's scythes flung down, and left in the half-cut swaths—Starbuck!

HERMAN MELVILLE, *Moby-Dick*, Chapter 132 (1851)

And so we are near the end.

Herman Melville, indefatigable poet that he was, allows Captain Ahab – as he closes in on his prey – a last moment of regret. For a moment he is far away from the killing field of the Pacific Ocean, 'under the slopes of the Andes', where 'the mowers are sleeping among the new-mown hay'. 'Sleeping?' 'Sleep?' For a moment, Ahab (like Robert Frost earlier, No. 66) considers sleep a possibility.

That, though, is not how the book will end.

When you cannot go further
It is time to go back and wrest
Out of the failure some
Thing shining.

As when a child I sat
On the stoop and spoke
The state licenses, the makes
Of autos going somewhere—

To others I leave the fleeting
Memory of myself.

DAVID SCHUBERT, 'No Finis' (1941)

That's what Ahab did momentarily, wrested 'Out of the failure some / Thing shining'. The Andes, the mowers, the new-mown hay.

And then he pressed on.

David Schubert doesn't press on. He sits on the stoop for a moment as when he was a child. As when, in a beautiful act of parroting, he 'spoke / The state licenses'.

But he doesn't end either. There is 'No finis'. 'To others I leave the fleeting / Memory of myself.' This, let's be honest, and no question, is one of the poet's objects: to leave a trace. Or at least, not to disappear without one:

143

However far back you go in your memory, it is always in some external, active manifestation of yourself that you come across your identity – in the work of your hands, in your family, in other people. And now look. You in others are yourself, your soul. This is what you are. This is what your consciousness has breathed and lived on and enjoyed throughout your life. Your soul, your immortality, your life in others.

BORIS PASTERNAK, *Doctor Zhivago*, Chapter 3 (1957), tr. Max Hayward and Manya Hari

The question: is the fleeting memory of oneself to be established through the life, or the work?

W.B. Yeats, as you will be aware, opted for the work:

144

The intellect of man is forced to choose
Perfection of the life, or of the work,
And if it take the second must refuse
A heavenly mansion, raging in the dark.

When all that story's finished, what's the news?
In luck or out the toil has left its mark:
That old perplexity an empty purse,
Or the day's vanity, the night's remorse.

W.B. YEATS, 'The Choice' (1933)

Curious, isn't it, the sense offered here of the perfected life, as if the perfection, in that respect, constituted a 'heavenly mansion' or an 'empty purse'?

Not that Yeats, who made his choice, considers one choice to be obviously more admirable than the other. 'Perfection of the work' equates, as the poem sees it, to 'the day's vanity, the night's remorse'.

Or consider this poem as rhyme: abababcc. Consider how the closing couplet closes the options down.

Time is short, we have to choose, and any one choice will preclude another. Yeats has become wise enough to know that no single choice is right.

145

Adieu, farewell earth's bliss,
This world uncertain is.
Fond are life's lustful joys –
Death proves them all but toys.
None from his darts can fly –
I am sick; I must die.
        Lord, have mercy on us.

Rich men, trust not in wealth:
Gold cannot buy you health;
Physic must fade:
All things to end are made.
The plague full swift goes by:
I am sick; I must die.
        Lord, have mercy on us.

Beauty is but a flower,
Which wrinkles will devour.
Brightness falls from the air;
Queens have died young and fair;
Dust hath closed Helen's eye:
I am sick; I must die.
        Lord, have mercy on us.

Strength stoops unto the grave;
Words feed on Hector brave;
Swords may not fight with fate;
Earth still holds ope her gate.
'Come, come' the bells do cry:
I am sick; I must die.
        Lord, have mercy on us.

Wit with his wantonness
Tasteth death's bitterness:
Hell's executioner
Hath no ears for to hear
What vain art can reply.
I am sick; I must die.
        Lord, have mercy on us.

Haste therefore each degree,
To welcome destiny.
Heaven is our heritage,
Earth but a players' stage;
Mount we unto the sky –
I am sick; I must die.
          Lord, have mercy on us.

THOMAS NASHE, 'In Time of Pestilence' (1600)

mercy n. 1 compassion or forgiveness shown towards an enemy or person in one's power. 2 something to be grateful for. 3 exclam. used to express surprise or fear.

As in 'small mercy', and 'Mercy me!' From the Old French *merci*, meaning pity or thanks.

As in, 'Lord, have mercy on us.'

146

Dark house, by which once more I stand
    Here in the long unlovely street,
    Doors, where my heart was used to beat
So quickly, waiting for a hand,

A hand that can be clasp'd no more—
    Behold me, for I cannot sleep,
    And like a guilty thing I creep
At earliest morning to the door.

He is not here; but far away
    The noise of life begins again,
    And ghastly through the drizzling rain
On the bald street breaks the blank day.

ALFRED LORD TENNYSON, from 'In Memoriam' (1850)

Tennyson again. 'Breaks' again. Here, though, even the 'break' is muted, 'blank'.

147

> Come, my friends,
> 'Tis not too late to seek a newer world.
> Push off, and sitting well in order smite
> The sounding furrows; for my purpose holds
> To sail beyond the sunset, and the baths
> Of all the western stars, until I die.
> It may be that the gulfs will wash us down:
> It may be we shall touch the Happy Isles,
> And see the great Achilles, whom we knew.
> Though much is taken, much abides; and though
> We are not now that strength which in old days
> Moved earth and heaven; that which we are, we are;
> One equal temper of heroic hearts,
> Made weak by time and fate, but strong in will,
> To strive, to seek, to find, and not to yield.

ALFRED LORD TENNYSON, from 'Ulysses' (1842)

Or:

148 So spake our mother Eve, and Adam heard
Well pleased, but answered not; for now too nigh
The archangel stood, and from the other hill
To their fixed station, all in bright array
The cherubim descended; on the ground
Gliding meteorous, as evening mist
Risen from a river o'er the marish glides,
And gathers ground fast as the labourer's heel
Homeward returning. High in front advanced,
The brandished sword of God before them blazed
Fierce as a comet; which with torrid heat,
And vapour as the Lybian air adust,
Began to parch that temperate clime; whereat
In either hand the hastening angel caught
Our lingering parents, and to the eastern gate
Led them direct, and down the cliff as fast
To the subjected plain; then disappeared.
They looking back, all the eastern side beheld
Of Paradise, so late their happy seat,
Waved over by that flaming brand, the gate
With dreadful faces thronged and fiery arms.
Some natural tears they dropped, but wiped them soon;
The world was all before them, where to choose
Their place of rest, and providence their guide:
They hand in hand, with wandering steps and slow,
Through Eden took their solitary way.

JOHN MILTON, *Paradise Lost*, Book 12, ll.624–49 (1674)

This is perhaps – we can't prove it, and nor do we want to – the most moving moment in all poetry, ever.

Having performed their disobedience, Adam and Eve are now banished from Eden, the 'brandished sword' marking their expulsion from their 'happy seat'.

And this would be unacceptable, which is to say all but unbearable, this loss of an environment so perfectly adjusted to human need, *were it not for the fact*, if we might say so at this terrible juncture, that the flaming sword is double-edged.

Because see what they now look out on: 'The world was all before them, where to choose / Their place of rest'. They have chosen badly already, they ate from the tree of knowledge, but still – no small mercy this – they have 'choice'.

What Milton presents, at the end of his poem, is free human agency.

Or to put it another way: possibilities.

149

As, finally, does Whitman:

The spotted hawk swoops by and accuses me .... he
    complains of my gab and my loitering.

I too am not a bit tamed .... I too am untranslatable,
I sound my barbaric yawp over the roofs of the world.

The last scud of day holds back for me,
It flings my likeness after the rest and true as any on the
    shadowed wilds,
It coaxes me to the vapor and the dusk.

I depart as air .... I shake my white locks at the runaway
    sun,
I effuse my flesh in eddies and drift it in lacy jags.

I bequeath myself to the dirt to grow from the grass I
    love,
If you want me again look for me under your bootsoles.

You will hardly know who I am or what I mean,
But I shall be good health to you nevertheless,
And filter and fibre your blood.

Failing to fetch me at first keep encouraged,
Missing me one place search another,
I stop some where waiting for you.

WALT WHITMAN, from 'Song of Myself' (1855)

Because, In all its strangeness and proto modernity, there is an
epic expulsion here too. These are the closing lines of Whitman's
most substantial poem, the poem he thought of as a kind of ur-
work of American literature, the basis of all future American poetic
expression.

Which makes him sound very dominant, very over-powering, a
poet, as James describes him, of mythic ego.

Except ... look carefully there, at the end of the poem. The principal
is not now 'I' but 'you'.

The reader, primed for his or her moment, has been released into
the world.

And that is entirely the point. Whitman's object was to make his readers 'fit', where 'fit' doesn't imply containment, but means ready, capable.

Ready for what? Capable of what?

Whatever. 'Fit' for their own purpose.

Read Milton: 'The world was all before them, where to choose ...'.

Epilogue

150 Past is past, and if one
remembers what one meant
to do and never did, is
not to have thought to do
enough? Like that gather-
ing of one of each I
planned, to gather one
of each kind of clover,
daisy, paintbrush that
grew in that field
the cabin stood in and
study them one afternoon
before they wilted. Past
is past. I salute
that various field.

JAMES SCHUYLER, 'Salute' (1969)

Us too: 'that various field'.

Index

References are to poem numbers, not page numbers.

Acknowledgements

The publisher wishes to thank the following for permission to reprint copyright material in this book, as listed below:

GUILLAUME APOLLINAIRE: 'La jolie rousse', tr. Robert Chandler from *20th-Century French Poems* (Faber & Faber, 2002), reprinted by permission of the translator; JOHN ASHBERY: 'And *Ut Pictura Poesis* Is Her Name' from *Houseboat Days* (Penguin Books, 1977); AMIRI BARAKA: 'Political Poem' from *Transbluesency: The Selected Poems of Amiri Baraka and Leroi Jones (1961–1995)* (Marsilio Publishers, 1995); GEORGES BATAILLE: extract, tr. Robert Hurley, from *Theory of Religion* (Zone Books, 1992), reprinted by permission of the publisher; JOHN BERRYMAN: 'Dream Song 14' from *The Dream Songs* (Faber & Faber, 1993); DAVID BOWMAN: extract from *fa fa fa fa fa fa: The Adventures of Talking Heads in the 20th Century* (Bloomsbury Publishing, 2001), reprinted by permission of the publisher; ANDRÉ BRETON: extract from 'Manifesto of Surrealism', tr. Richard Seaver and Helen R. Lane, from *Manifestoes of Surrealism* (University of Michigan Press, 1969); BASIL BUNTING: 'On the Fly-Leaf of Pound's Cantos' from *Complete Poems* (Bloodaxe Books, 2000), reprinted by permission of the publisher; PAUL CELAN: 'Todesfugue', tr. Michael Hamburger, from *Poems of Paul Celan*, third edition (Anvil Press Poetry, 2007), reprinted by permission of the publisher; T.S. ELIOT: extract from 'Tradition and the Individual Talent' (1919) from *The Best American Essays* (Mariner Books, 2001); extract from *The Use of Poetry and the Use of Criticism: Studies in the relation of criticism to poetry*, second/revised edition (Faber & Faber, 1987); WILLIAM EMPSON: extract from *Seven Types of Ambiguity* (Pimlico, 2004), reprinted by permission of The Random House Group Ltd; and extracts from *The Complete Poems of William Empson* (Allen Lane, 2000); ROBERT FROST: 'After Apple-Picking' from *The Collected Poems of Robert Frost* (Henry Holt, 1969), reprinted by permission of The Random House Group Ltd; ALLEN GINSBERG: 'A Supermarket in California' from *Selected Poems 1947–1995* (Penguin Twentieth-Century Classics, 1997); IVOR GURNEY: 'The Escape' from *Collected Poems* (Carcanet Press, 2004), reprinted by permission of the publisher; GEOFFREY HILL: 'Ovid in the Third Reich' from *Collected Poems* (Penguin International Poets, 1985); LANGSTON HUGHES: 'The Negro Speaks of Rivers' from *The Collected Poems of Langston Hughes* (Alfred A. Knopf, 1994), reprinted by permission of David Higham Associates Ltd; LEWIS HYDE: extract from *The Gift: Imagination and the Erotic Life of Property* (Vintage Books, 1988); LINTON KWESI JOHNSON: 'Di Great Insohreckshan' from *Selected Poems* (Penguin Books, 2006); PHILIP LARKIN: extract from 'Money' from *Collected Poems*

(Faber & Faber, 1990); DENISE LEVERTOV: 'Action' from *Selected Poems* (New Directions, 2003), reprinted by permission of Pollinger Ltd and the proprietor; HUGH MACDIARMID: 'My Ambition' from *Complete Poems* (Penguin Modern Classics, 1985), reprinted by permission of Carcanet Press; LOUIS MACNEICE: 'The Taxis' from *Collected Poems* (Faber & Faber, 1979), reprinted by permission of David Higham Associates; JOHN MASEFIELD: 'Cargoes' from *Collected Poems* (William Heinemann, 1924), reprinted by permission of The Society of Authors as the Literary Representative of the Estate of John Masefield; MARIANNE MOORE: 'When I Buy Pictures' from *Complete Poems* (Faber & Faber, 1984); LORINE NIEDECKER: 'In Leonardo's light', 'You are my friend' and 'Nursery Rhyme' from *Lorine Niedecker: Collected Works* (University of California Press, 2004); FRANK O'HARA: 'Poem', 'Poem', 'Radio' and 'Why I am not a painter' from *The Collected Poems of Frank O'Hara* (Random House, 1988); CHARLES OLSON: 'May 31, 1961' from *The Collected Poems of Charles Olson* (University of California Press, 1992); 'Projective Verse' from *Collected Prose* (University of California Press, 1997); GEORGE OPPEN: 'Sara in Her Father's Arms' from *Collected Poems* (W.W. Norton, 1975); EZRA POUND: 'Vorticism' from *Gaudier-Brzeska: A Memoir* (W.W. Norton, 1974); 'The Garden' from *Selected Poems 1908–1969* (Faber & Faber, 1977); 'Canto XLIX' from *The Cantos of Ezra Pound* (New Directions, 1996); 'Ancient Music' from *Personae: The Shorter Poems of Ezra Pound* (New Directions, 1990), copyright (c) 1926 by Ezra Pound, reprinted by permission of the publisher; PIERRE REVERDY: extract from *Les Ardoises du Toit*, tr. Patricia Terry, from *Roof Slates and Other Poems of Pierre Reverdy* (Northeastern University Press, 1981); I.A. RICHARDS: extract from *Practical Criticism: A Study of Literary Judgement* (Routledge, 1929); MURIEL RUKEYSER: 'Homage to Literature' from *Collected Poems of Muriel Rukeyser* (University of Pittsburgh Press, 2006); DAVID SCHUBERT: 'No Finis' from *Works and Days* from *Quarterly Review of Literature*, Volume 24; JAMES SCHUYLER: 'Stun' and 'Salute' from *Collected Poems* (Farrar, Straus & Giroux, 1993); WILLIAM STAFFORD: 'Traveling Through The Dark' from *Stories that could be true: New and collected poems* (Harper & Row, 1977); GERTRUDE STEIN: extract from *Tender Buttons* (Alan Rodgers Books, 2006), reprinted by permission of David Higham Associates; WALLACE STEVENS: extracts from 'Sunday Morning' and 'Evening without Angels' from *Collected Poems of Wallace Stevens* (Faber & Faber, 2006); JAMES THURBER: 'The Tyranny of Trivia' from *Lanterns and Lances* (Hamish Hamilton, 1961); PAUL VALÉRY: 'Au Soleil', tr. Stephen Romer, from *20th-Century French Poems* (Faber & Faber, 2002); JOHN WIENERS: 'Espionage' and 'Times Square' from *Nerves* (Cape Goliard, 1971); WILLIAM CARLOS WILLIAMS: 'To Elsie' from *Collected Poems of William Carlos Williams* (Carcanet Press, 2000), reprinted by permission of the publisher; W.B. YEATS: 'Spilt Milk' and 'The Choice' from *Collected Poems* (Picador, 1990); LOUIS ZUKOFSKY: extract from *A Useful Art: Essays and Radio Scripts on American Design* (Wesleyan University Press, 2003); STEFAN ZWEIG: extract from *Confusion*, tr. Anthea Bell (Pushkin Press, 2002).

Every effort has been made to establish copyright and contact copyright holders prior to publication. However, the publishers will be glad to rectify in future editions any inadvertent omissions or errors brought to their attention.